TIMED READINGS
in Literature
BOOK FIVE

Edward Spargo, Editor

Selections & Questions
for this Edition:
Henry Billings
Melissa Billings

Fifty 400-Word Passages
with Questions for
Building Reading Speed

Jamestown Publishers

Titles in This Series
Timed Readings, Third Edition
Timed Readings in Literature

Teaching Notes are available for this text and
will be sent to the instructor. Please write on
school stationery; tell us what grade
you teach and identify the text.

Timed Readings in Literature

Catalog No. 915

© 1989 by Jamestown Publishers, Inc.

Cover and text design by Deborah Hulsey Christie

Printed in the United States of America

4 5 6 7 GG 99 98 97 96

ISBN 0-89061-518-7

Contents

Introduction to the Student   4

Reading Literature Faster   8

How to Use This Book   12

Instructions for the Pacing Drills   14

Timed Reading Selections   15

Answer Key   116

Progress Graph   118

Pacing Graph   120

Introduction to the Student

These *Timed Readings in Literature* are designed to help you become a faster and better reader. As you progress through the book, you will find yourself growing in reading speed and comprehension. You will be challenged to increase your reading rate while maintaining a high level of comprehension.

Reading, like most things, improves with practice. If you practice improving your reading speed, you will improve. As you will see, the rewards of improved reading speed will be well worth your time and effort.

Why Read Faster?

The quick and simple answer is that faster readers are better readers. Does this statement surprise you? You might think that fast readers would miss something and their comprehension might suffer. This is not true, for two reasons:

1. Faster readers comprehend faster. When you read faster, the writer's message is coming to you faster and makes sense sooner. Ideas are interconnected. The writer's thoughts are all tied together, each one leading to the next. The more quickly you can see how ideas are related to each other, the more quickly you can comprehend the meaning of what you are reading.

2. Faster readers concentrate better. Concentration is essential for comprehension. If your mind is wandering you can't understand what you are reading. A lack of concentration causes you to re-read, sometimes over and over, in order to comprehend. Faster readers concentrate better because there's less time for distractions to interfere. Comprehension, in turn, contributes to concentration. If you are concentrating and comprehending, you will not become distracted.

Want to Read More?

Do you wish that you could read more? (or, at least, would you like to do your required reading in less time?) Faster reading will help.

The illustration on the next page shows the number of books someone might read over a period of ten years. Let's see what faster reading could

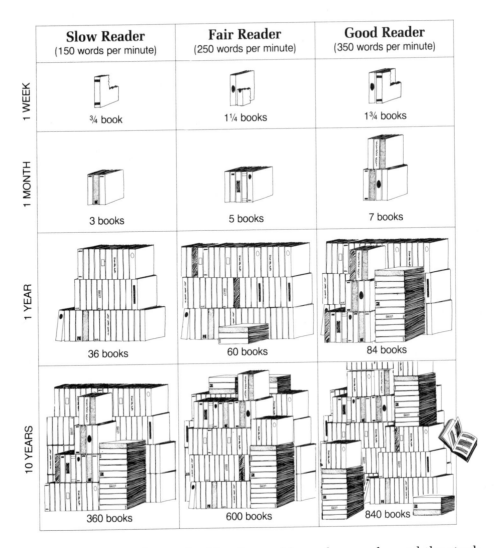

	Slow Reader (150 words per minute)	Fair Reader (250 words per minute)	Good Reader (350 words per minute)
1 WEEK	¾ book	1¼ books	1¾ books
1 MONTH	3 books	5 books	7 books
1 YEAR	36 books	60 books	84 books
10 YEARS	360 books	600 books	840 books

do for you. Look at the stack of books read by a slow reader and the stack read by a good reader. (We show a speed of 350 words a minute for our "good" reader, but many fast readers can more than double that speed.) Let's say, however, that you are now reading at a rate of 150 words a minute. The illustration shows you reading 36 books a year. By increasing your reading speed to 250 words a minute, you could increase the number of books to 60 a year.

We have arrived at these numbers by assuming that the readers in our illustration read for one hour a day, six days a week, and that an average book is about 72,000 words long. Many people do not read that much, but they might if they could learn to read better and faster.

Faster reading doesn't *take* time, it *saves* time!

Acquisitional *vs.* Recreational Reading

Timed Readings in Literature gives practice in a certain kind of reading: recreational reading. Recreational reading of novels and short stories is different from the kind of reading you must employ with textbooks. You read a textbook to *acquire* facts and information. That is acquisitional reading, reading that is careful and deliberate—you cannot afford to miss something you may be quizzed on later. Acquisitional reading speed must be slower than recreational reading speed.

The practice you will be doing in this book will help you develop a high reading speed suitable for literature.

Why Practice on Literature?

If acquisitional reading is so useful and important for students, why should you spend valuable class time learning to read literature faster? Shouldn't you be learning to read textbooks faster and better? Believe it or not, you are! That's right: the reading speed and skills you develop from this book will transfer to your textbooks and to other study reading. Here are some of the ways this happens.

1. The practice effect. In the dictionary, *practice* is defined as systematic exercise to gain proficiency. In other words, repeated drill brings improvement. You know from your own experience that when you practice anything—from piano to basketball—you become better at it. The same holds true for reading. As you are doing the drills and exercises in these books, you are practicing *all* of your reading skills at the same time. With practice you become a fluent reader and comprehender—a better reader of everything you read.

2. Using context. Good readers are aware of context and use it to aid understanding. Context refers to the words surrounding those you are reading. Meaning, you see, does not come from a single word, or even a single sentence—it is conveyed within the whole context of what you are reading.

The language of literature is rich with meaning. The storyteller is trying to *please* the reader, not *teach* the reader. The writer wants to share feelings and experiences with the reader, to reach him or her in a personal way. As you practice reading literature, you are developing your skill in using context to extract the full measure of meaning and appreciation. These same context skills can be put to work when you are reading textbooks to help you organize facts into a meaningful body of knowledge.

3. Vocabulary growth. Our early vocabulary comes from listening—to our families, friends, television, teachers, and classmates. We learn and understand new words as we hear them being used by others. In fact, the more times we encounter a word, the better we understand it. Finally, it becomes ours, part of our permanent vocabulary of words we know and use.

As time goes by, an increasing number of words is introduced to us through recreational reading. Most of the words we know come from reading—words we have never looked up in a dictionary, but whose meanings have become clear to us through seeing them again and again until they are finally ours. Literature, the kind you will be reading in this book, provides countless opportunities for meeting and learning new words. Literature, as you have seen, also provides the context for seeing these new words used with precision and effect. As you work through the pages in this book, you will be developing a larger and stronger vocabulary—a storehouse of words that become your tools for learning.

4. Skills transfer. You are using this book to develop your ability to read literature with increased speed and comprehension. With regular practice and a little effort, you will be successful in reaching that goal.

As we mentioned, you will also be improving your context skills and building a bigger vocabulary. These are all wonderful results from using this book.

But, perhaps the greatest benefit of all is the application of these improvements to all of your reading tasks, not just literature. Using this book will make you a better reader, and *better readers read everything better.*

Reading Literature Faster

Through literature we share an experience with a writer. That experience may be presented as a conversation, a character or scene, an emotion, or an event.

Let's examine these four kinds of presentation. Let's see if there are characteristics or clues we can use to help us identify each kind. Once we know what we are expected to experience, we can read more intelligently and more quickly.

When you are working in this book, your instructor will schedule a few moments for you to preview each selection before timing begins. Use the preview time to scan the selection rapidly, looking for one of the following kinds of presentation.

1. Reading and Understanding a Conversation

A conversation is intended to tell us what characters are thinking or feeling—the best way to do this is through their own words.

Read the following conversation between George and his mother, an excerpt from "George's Mother" by Stephen Crane:

> Finally he said savagely: "Damn these early hours!" His mother jumped as if he had thrown a missile at her. "Why, George—" she began.
>
> George broke in again. "Oh, I know all that—but this gettin' up in th' mornin' so early just makes me sick. Jest when a man is gettin' his mornin' nap he's gotta get up. I—"
>
> "George, dear," said his mother, "yeh know I hate yeh to swear, dear. Now, please don't." She looked beseechingly at him.
>
> He made a swift gesture. "Well, I ain't swearin', am I?" he demanded. "I was only sayin' that this gettin'-up business gives me a pain, wasn't I?"
>
> "Well, yeh know how swearin' hurts me," protested the little old woman. She seemed about to sob. She gazed off . . . apparently recalling persons who had never been profane.

First, is this a conversation? Yes, we know it is. There are quotation marks throughout indicating words spoken by the characters. So, to identify a conversation, we look for quotation marks.

Next, does this conversation tell us what the characters are thinking or feeling? It certainly does—this conversation is unmistakably clear. We know how George *feels* about getting up in the morning, and we know how his mother *feels* about profanity.

Finally, how should we read this and other conversations we encounter in literature? Join the conversation; pretend you are one of the speakers and that these are your own words. Listen to the other character as though words are being addressed to you.

Conversations can be read quickly and understood well when you recognize them and become part of them.

2. Reading About and Understanding a Character or Scene

How do we learn about a character? There are many ways. Writers introduce characters (1) by telling us what they look like; (2) by what they say; (3) by the things they do; and (4) by telling us what others think and say about them:

> He was a staid, placid gentleman, something past the prime of life, yet upright in his carriage for all that, and slim as a greyhound. He was well mounted upon a sturdy chestnut cob, and had the graceful seat of an experienced horseman; while his riding gear, though free from such fopperies as were then in vogue, was handsome and well chosen. He wore a riding coat of a somewhat brighter green than might have been expected to suit the taste of a gentleman of his years, with a short, black velvet cape, and laced pocket holes and cuffs, all of a jaunty fashion; his linen too, was of the finest kind, worked in a rich pattern at the wrists and throat, and scrupulously white. Although he seemed, judging from the mud he had picked up on the way, to have come from London, his horse was as smooth and cool as his own iron-gray periwig and pigtail.

Obviously a character is being introduced to us in this passage from *Barnaby Rudge* by Charles Dickens. We are told how he carries himself and how he is dressed. We even know a little about what he has been doing.

The question to ask yourself is: Is this character lifelike and real? Real characters should be like real people—good and bad, happy and sad, alike and different. In reading about characters, look for the same details you look for in all people.

Similarly, when a scene or location is being described, look for words which tell about size, shape, color, appearance. Such descriptor words help us picture in our minds the place being described. Try to visualize the scene as you read.

3. Experiencing an Emotion Through Literature

When a writer presents an emotion for us to experience, the intent is to produce an effect within us. The intended effect may be pity, fear, revulsion, or some other emotion. The writer wants us to *feel* something.

In the following passage from *Jane Eyre* by Charlotte Brontë, what emotions are we expected to feel for the character?

> John had not much affection for his mother and sisters, and an antipathy to me. He bullied and punished me; not two or three times in the week, not once or twice in the day, but continually: every nerve I had feared him, and every morsel of flesh on my bones shrank when he came near. There were moments when I was bewildered by the terror he inspired, because I had no appeal whatever against either his menaces or his inflictions; the servants did not like to offend their young master by taking my part against him, and Mrs. Reed was blind and deaf on the subject: She never saw him strike or heard him abuse me, though he did both now and then in her very presence; more frequently behind her back.

Do you feel sorry for this girl because she is being abused? Do you feel compassion because she is suffering? Are you suffering with her? Do you feel anger toward her abuser? What other effects are intended? How are these effects produced?

Emotional and provocative words and expressions have been employed by the writer to paint a vivid portrait of her character's predicament. Can you identify some of the words? What did John do? He *bullied, struck, punished,* and *abused*. The girl felt fear, bewilderment, and terror. These very expressive and emotional words and phrases are the clues provided by the writer to help her readers read and comprehend effectively.

4. Reading About and Understanding an Event

In describing an event—a series of actions—the writer is telling us a story, and the elements of the story are presented in some kind of order or pattern. Read this passage from *Around the World in Eighty Days* by Jules Verne:

> Mr. Fogg and his two companions took their places on a bench opposite the desks of the magistrate and his clerk. Immediately after, Judge Obadiah, a fat, round man, followed by the clerk, entered. He proceeded to take down a wig which was hanging on a nail, and put it hurriedly on his head.
>
> "The first case," said he. Then, putting his hand to his head, he exclaimed "Heh! This is not my wig!"
>
> "No, your worship," returned the clerk, "it is mine."
>
> "My dear Mr. Oysterpuff, how can a judge give a wise sentence in a clerk's wig?"
>
> The wigs were exchanged.

Did you see how this little story was told? The events in the story were presented in chronological order—from first to last as they occurred. This is a frequently used and easily recognized pattern, but not the only one writers use. The story could have been told in reverse—the story could have opened with the judge wearing the wrong wig and then gone on to explain how the mistake happened.

In passages like these, look for the events in the story and see how they are related, how one event follows or builds on the other. By recognizing the pattern of storytelling and using the pattern as an aid to organizing and understanding the events, you can become a better and faster reader.

How to Use This Book

1 Read the lessons
First, read the lessons on pages 8 through 11. These lessons teach you how to recognize and identify the kinds of presentation you encounter in literature and in the selections in this book.

2 Preview
Find a literature selection to read and wait for your instructor's signal to preview. You will have 30 seconds to preview (scan) the selection to identify the author's kind of presentation.

3 Begin reading
When your instructor gives you the signal, begin reading. Read at a slightly faster-than-normal speed. Read well enough so that you will be able to answer questions about what you have read.

7 Fill in the progress graph
Enter your score and plot your reading time on the graph on page 118 or 119. The right-hand side of the graph shows your words-per-minute reading speed. Write this number at the bottom of the page on the line labeled *Words per Minute.*

4 Record your time

When you finish reading, look at the blackboard and note your reading time. Your reading time will be the lowest time remaining on the board, or the next number to be erased. Write this time at the bottom of the page on the line labeled *Reading Time*.

5 Answer the questions

Answer the ten questions on the next page. There are five fact questions and five thought questions. Pick the *best* answer to each question and put an x in the box beside it.

6 Correct your answers

Using the Answer Key on pages 116 and 117, correct your work. Circle your wrong answers and put an x in the box you should have marked. Score 10 points for each correct answer. Write your score at the bottom of the page on the line labeled *Comprehension Score*.

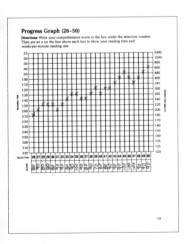

Instructions for the Pacing Drills

From time to time your instructor may wish to conduct pacing drills using *Timed Readings*. For this work you need to use the Pacing Dots printed in the margins of your book pages. The dots will help you regulate your reading speed to match the pace set by your instructor or announced on the reading cassette tape.

Pacing Dots

You will be reading at the correct pace if you are at the dot when your instructor says "Mark" or when you hear a tone on the tape. If you are ahead of the pace, read a little more slowly; if you are behind the pace, increase your reading speed. Try to match the pace exactly.

Follow these steps.

Step 1: Record the pace. At the bottom of the page, write on the line labeled *Words per Minute* the rate announced by the instructor or by the speaker on the tape.

Step 2: Begin reading. Wait for the signal to begin reading. Read at a slightly faster-than-normal speed. You will not know how on-target your pace is until you hear your instructor say "Mark" or until you hear the first tone on the tape. After a little practice you will be able to select an appropriate starting speed most of the time.

Step 3: Adjust your pace. As you read, try to match the pace set by the instructor or the tape. Read more slowly or more quickly as necessary. You should be reading the line beside the dot when you hear the pacing signal. The pacing sounds may distract you at first. Don't worry about it. Keep reading and your concentration will return.

Step 4: Stop and answer questions. Stop reading when you are told to, even if you have not finished the selection. Answer the questions right away. Correct your work and record your score on the line *Comprehension Score*. Strive to maintain 80 percent comprehension on each drill as you gradually increase your pace.

Step 5: Fill in the pacing graph. Transfer your words-per-minute rate to the box labeled *Pace* on the pacing graph on page 120. Then plot your comprehension score on the line above the box.

These pacing drills are designed to help you become a more flexible reader. They encourage you to "break out" of a pattern of reading everything at the same speed.

The drills help in other ways, too. Sometimes in a reading program you reach a certain level and bog down. You don't seem able to move on and progress. The pacing drills will help you to work your way out of such slumps and get your reading program moving again.

from **Little Women** *by Louisa May Alcott*

"I've done my best, but you *won't* be reasonable, and it's selfish of you to keep teasing for what I can't give. I shall always be fond of you, very fond indeed, as a friend, but I'll never marry you!"

That speech was like fire to gunpowder. Laurie looked at her a minute as if he did not quite know what to do with himself, then turned sharply away, saying in a desperate sort of tone, "You'll be sorry someday, Jo."

"Oh, where are you going?" she cried, for his face frightened her.

"To the devil!" was the consoling answer.

For a minute Jo's heart stood still, as he swung himself down the bank toward the river, but it takes much folly, sin or misery to send a young man to a violent death, and Laurie was not one of the weak sort who are conquered by a single failure. He had no thought of a melodramatic plunge, but some blind instinct led him to fling hat and coat into his boat, and row away with all his might, making better time up the river than he had done in many a race. Jo drew a long breath and unclasped her hands as she watched the poor fellow trying to outstrip the trouble which he carried in his heart.

"That will do him good, and he'll come home in such a tender, penitent state of mind, that I shan't dare to see him," she said, adding, as she went slowly home, feeling as if she had murdered some innocent thing, and buried it under the leaves, "Now I must go and prepare Mr. Laurence to be very kind to my poor boy. I wish he'd love Beth, perhaps he may in time, but I begin to think I was mistaken about her. Oh dear! How can girls like to have lovers and refuse them. I think it's dreadful."

Being sure that no one could do it so well as herself, she went straight to Mr. Laurence, told the hard story bravely through, and then broke down, crying so dismally over her own insensibility that the kind old gentleman, though sorely disappointed, did not utter a reproach. He found it difficult to understand how any girl could help loving Laurie, and hoped she would change her mind, but he knew even better than Jo that love cannot be forced.

Recalling Facts

1. Jo turned down Laurie's
   - ☐ a. marriage proposal.
   - ☐ b. wedding invitation.
   - ☐ c. dinner engagement.

2. Jo said Laurie was not being
   - ☐ a. helpful.
   - ☐ b. passionate.
   - ☐ c. reasonable.

3. Laurie told Jo that someday she would be
   - ☐ a. happy.
   - ☐ b. sorry.
   - ☐ c. married.

4. After leaving Jo, Laurie
   - ☐ a. got into a rowboat.
   - ☐ b. ran down the street.
   - ☐ c. swam across the river.

5. Jo told her story first to
   - ☐ a. Beth.
   - ☐ b. Mr. Laurence.
   - ☐ c. Laurie's mother.

Understanding the Passage

6. Laurie reacted to Jo's rejection by
   - ☐ a. calmly walking away.
   - ☐ b. breaking down in tears.
   - ☐ c. warning her.

7. Laurie was not the sort of man to
   - ☐ a. commit suicide.
   - ☐ b. get angry.
   - ☐ c. fall in love.

8. Laurie apparently enjoyed
   - ☐ a. rowboat racing.
   - ☐ b. long walks.
   - ☐ c. going upriver.

9. After Laurie left, Jo felt
   - ☐ a. joyous.
   - ☐ b. guilty.
   - ☐ c. lonely.

10. Mr. Laurence couldn't understand why
    - ☐ a. Laurie broke down.
    - ☐ b. marriages were not arranged by parents.
    - ☐ c. any girl would reject Laurie.

from **The Posthumous Papers
of the Pickwick Club** *by Charles Dickens*

Twenty years ago, that pavement was worn with the footsteps of a mother and child, who, day by day, so surely as the morning came, presented themselves at the prison gate. Often after a night of restless misery and anxious thoughts, they were there, a full hour too soon. Then the young mother, turning meekly away, would lead the child to the old bridge, and raising him in her arms to show him the glistening water, tinted with the light of the morning's sun, and stirring with all the bustling preparations for business and pleasure, endeavor to interest his thoughts in the objects before him. But she would quickly set him down, and hiding her face in her shawl, give vent to the tears that blinded her; for no expression of interest or amusement lighted up his thin and sickly face. His recollections were few enough, but they were all of one kind: all connected with the poverty and misery of his parents. Hour after hour he had sat on his mother's knee, and with childish sympathy watched the tears that stole down her face, and then crept quietly away into some dark corner, and sobbed himself to sleep. The hard realities of the world, with many of its worst privations—hunger and thirst, and cold and want—had all come home to him, from the first dawnings of reason; and though the form of childhood was there, its light heart, its merry laugh, and sparkling eyes, were wanting.

The father and mother looked upon this with thoughts of agony they dared not breathe in words. The healthy, strong-made man, who could have borne almost any fatigue of active exertion, was wasting beneath the close confinement and unhealthy atmosphere of a crowded prison. The slight and delicate woman was sinking beneath the combined effects of bodily and mental illness. The child's young heart was breaking.

Winter came, and with it weeks of cold and heavy rain. The poor girl had removed to a wretched apartment close to the spot of her husband's imprisonment. Although the change had been rendered necessary by their increasing poverty, she was happier now, for she was nearer him. For two months, she and her little companion watched the opening of the gate as usual. One day she failed to come, for the first time. Another morning arrived, and she came alone. The child was dead.

Recalling Facts

1. Every day, the mother and child came to the
   □ a. prison gate.
   □ b. hospital entrance.
   □ c. village shops.

2. Often the mother and child arrived
   □ a. before the gates opened.
   □ b. in the heat of midday.
   □ c. just as the gates were closing.

3. The child's life was filled with
   □ a. love and happiness.
   □ b. poverty and misery.
   □ c. violence and abuse.

4. The mother was suffering from
   □ a. physical illness.
   □ b. mental illness.
   □ c. both a and b.

5. The child died during the
   □ a. summer.
   □ b. winter.
   □ c. fall.

Understanding the Passage

6. The parents knew their child was
   □ a. suffering from his hard life.
   □ b. very intelligent.
   □ c. having trouble in school.

7. While waiting to see her husband, the mother often tried to
   □ a. send him a message.
   □ b. plead with the guards.
   □ c. amuse her child.

8. When the mother thought of her child's sickly state, she
   □ a. decided to call a doctor.
   □ b. blamed her husband.
   □ c. broke down and cried.

9. The mother apparently
   □ a. loved her child very much.
   □ b. often left her child alone.
   □ c. had once been wealthy.

10. The child spent many hours
    □ a. visiting his father.
    □ b. out on the water.
    □ c. playing with his friends.

It was not the afternoon to be on deck—on the contrary, it was exactly the afternoon when there is no snugger place than a warm cabin, a warm bunk. Tucked up with a rug, a hot-water bottle and a piping hot cup of tea she would not have minded the weather in the least. But he hated cabins, hated to be inside anywhere more than was absolutely necessary. He had a passion for keeping, as he called it, above board, especially when he was traveling. And it wasn't surprising, considering the enormous amount of time he spent cooped up in the office. So, when he rushed away from her as soon as they got on board and came back five minutes later to say he had secured two deck chairs on the lee side and the steward was undoing the rugs, her voice through the high sealskin collar murmured "Good"; and because he was looking at her, she smiled with bright eyes and blinked quickly, as if to say, "Yes, perfectly all right—absolutely." And she meant it.

"Then we'd better—" said he, and he tucked her hand inside his arm and began to hurry her off to where their chairs stood. She just had time to breathe, "Not so fast, please," when he remembered too and slowed down.

Strange! They had been married twenty-eight years, and it was still an effort to him, each time, to adapt his pace to hers.

"Not cold, are you?" he asked, glancing sideways at her. Her little nose, geranium pink above the dark fur, was answer enough. But she thrust her free hand into the velvet pocket of her jacket and murmured gaily, "I shall be glad of my rug."

He knew, of course, that she ought to be down in the cabin; it was no afternoon for her to be sitting on deck, in this cold and raw mist, and he realized how she must be hating it. But he had come to believe that it really was easier for her to make these sacrifices than it was for him. If he had gone down to the cabin with her, he would have been miserable the whole time, and he couldn't have helped showing it. Whereas, having made up her mind to fall in with his ideas, he would have betted anybody she would even go so far as to enjoy the experience.

Recalling Facts

1. The husband in the
   passage hated
   - ☐ a. his life.
   - ☐ b. small ships.
   - ☐ c. to be inside.

2. The husband worked
   - ☐ a. for the steward.
   - ☐ b. as a traveling salesman.
   - ☐ c. in an office.

3. The couple had been married
   - ☐ a. twenty years.
   - ☐ b. twenty-six years.
   - ☐ c. twenty-eight years.

4. The wife was wearing a
   coat with a
   - ☐ a. geranium pinned to it.
   - ☐ b. row of shiny brass
     buttons on it.
   - ☐ c. sealskin collar.

5. On the lee side, the husband
   had found
   - ☐ a. a shop that served
     hot tea.
   - ☐ b. a hot-water bottle
     and a rug.
   - ☐ c. two deck chairs.

Understanding the Passage

6. The husband found
   the weather
   - ☐ a. freezing.
   - ☐ b. too humid.
   - ☐ c. pleasant.

7. Most people on board the
   ship spent this afternoon
   - ☐ a. on the lee side.
   - ☐ b. inside.
   - ☐ c. in the dining area.

8. The husband and
   wife walked
   - ☐ a. at different paces.
   - ☐ b. very slowly.
   - ☐ c. extremely fast.

9. The wife was trying to
   - ☐ a. start an argument.
   - ☐ b. be agreeable.
   - ☐ c. talk to the steward.

10. The wife wanted to
    - ☐ a. be with her husband.
    - ☐ b. have some time alone.
    - ☐ c. meet as many people as
      possible.

About this time the question of having some kind of a school opened for the colored children in the village began to be discussed by members of the race. As it would be the first school for Negro children that had ever been opened in that part of Virginia, it was, of course, to be a great event, and the discussion excited the widest interest. The most perplexing question was where to find a teacher. The young man from Ohio who had learned to read the papers was considered, but his age was against him. In the midst of the discussion about a teacher, another young colored man from Ohio, who had been a soldier, in some way found his way into town. It was soon learned that he possessed considerable education, and he was engaged by the colored people to teach their first school. As yet no free schools had been started for colored people in that section, hence each family agreed to pay a certain amount per month, with the understanding that the teacher was to "board 'round"—that is, spend a day with each family. This was not bad for the teacher, for each family tried to provide the very best on the day the teacher was to be its guest. I recall that I looked forward with an anxious appetite to the "teacher's day" at our little cabin.

This experience of a whole race beginning to go to school for the first time presents one of the most interesting studies that has ever occurred in connection with the development of any race. Few people who were not right in the midst of the scene can form any exact idea of the intense desire which the people of my race showed for an education. As I have stated, it was a whole race trying to go to school. Few were too young, and none too old, to make the attempt to learn. As fast as any kind of teachers could be secured, not only were day schools filled, but night schools as well. The great ambition of the older people was to try to learn to read the Bible before they died. With this end in view, men and women who were fifty or seventy-five years old would often be found in the night school. Day school, night school, Sunday school were always crowded, and often many had to be turned away for want of room.

Recalling Facts

1. The school mentioned in the passage was the area's first
   □ a. school for blacks.
   □ b. parish school.
   □ c. school for children.

2. The school's first teacher was
   □ a. a young married woman.
   □ b. an ex-soldier from Ohio.
   □ c. seventy-five years old.

3. The families agreed to let the teacher
   □ a. "board 'round."
   □ b. live in the church basement.
   □ c. work without pay.

4. The older people wanted to learn
   □ a. addition and subtraction.
   □ b. skills for farming.
   □ c. to read the Bible.

5. Many people were turned away from the school for lack of
   □ a. room.
   □ b. training.
   □ c. interest.

Understanding the Passage

6. The narrator lived in
   □ a. Ohio.
   □ b. a little cabin.
   □ c. the teacher's home.

7. The blacks in the area were
   □ a. reluctant to attend school.
   □ b. too busy to attend school.
   □ c. eager to attend school.

8. The students at the school were
   □ a. mostly young children.
   □ b. all male.
   □ c. of all ages.

9. Some classes were taught
   □ a. by children.
   □ b. at night.
   □ c. by whites.

10. Before the school opened, most blacks
    □ a. could not read.
    □ b. were indifferent to education.
    □ c. sent their children away to school.

The spring day cheered even me by the loveliness of its sunshine and the balminess of the air. I felt emotions of gentleness and pleasure, that had long appeared dead, revive within me. I allowed myself to be borne away by them; and, forgetting my solitude and deformity, dared to be happy. Soft tears again bedewed my cheeks, and I even raised my humid eyes with thankfulness toward the blessed sun which bestowed such joy upon me.

I continued to wind among the paths of the wood, until I came to its boundary, which was skirted by a deep and rapid river, into which many of the trees bent their branches, now budding with the fresh spring. Here I paused, not exactly knowing what path to pursue, when I heard the sound of voices that induced me to conceal myself under the shade of a cypress. I was scarcely hid, when a young girl came running toward the spot where I was concealed, laughing, as if she ran from someone in sport. She continued her course along the precipitous sides of the river, when suddenly her foot slipped, and she fell into the rapid stream. I rushed from my hiding place; and, with extreme labor from the force of the current, saved her, and dragged her to shore. She was senseless; and I endeavored by every means in my power to restore animation, when I was suddenly interrupted by the approach of a rustic, who was probably the person from whom she had playfully fled. On seeing me, he darted toward me, and tearing the girl from my arms, hastened toward the deeper parts of the wood. I followed speedily, I hardly knew why; but when the man saw me draw near, he aimed a gun, which he carried, at my body, and fired. I sunk to the ground, and my injurer escaped into the wood.

This was then the reward of my benevolence! I had saved a human being from destruction, and, as a recompense, I now writhed under the miserable pain of a wound, which shattered the flesh and bone. The feelings of kindness and gentleness which I had entertained but a few moments before gave place to hellish rage and gnashing of teeth. Inflamed by pain, I vowed eternal hatred and vengeance to all mankind. But the agony of my wound overcame me; my pulse paused, and I fainted.

Recalling Facts

1. The narrator was out on a
   - ☐ a. bright winter day.
   - ☐ b. cloudy spring day.
   - ☐ c. sunny spring day.

2. The narrator was
   - ☐ a. climbing a mountain.
   - ☐ b. walking in the woods.
   - ☐ c. lying under a cypress tree.

3. A young girl came running toward the narrator
   - ☐ a. crying.
   - ☐ b. laughing.
   - ☐ c. screaming.

4. The narrator saved the young girl from
   - ☐ a. drowning.
   - ☐ b. being shot.
   - ☐ c. getting lost.

5. As a reward for helping the young girl, the narrator was
   - ☐ a. warmly embraced.
   - ☐ b. chased by a stranger.
   - ☐ c. shot by a rustic.

Understanding the Passage

6. The narrator had been
   - ☐ a. bitter and lonely for some time.
   - ☐ b. enjoying a run of good luck.
   - ☐ c. well liked by many people.

7. When the narrator heard voices, he wanted to
   - ☐ a. hide himself.
   - ☐ b. greet the strangers.
   - ☐ c. run away.

8. The rustic seems to have been afraid of the
   - ☐ a. narrator.
   - ☐ b. girl.
   - ☐ c. river.

9. The rustic can best be described as
   - ☐ a. careless.
   - ☐ b. appreciative.
   - ☐ c. ungrateful.

10. Apparently the wound sustained by the narrator was
    - ☐ a. healing quickly.
    - ☐ b. serious but not fatal.
    - ☐ c. the cause of his death.

from **20,000 Leagues under the Sea** *by Jules Verne*

Captain Farragut was a good seaman, worthy of the frigate he commanded. His vessel and he were one. He was the soul of it. On the question of the cetacean there was no doubt in his mind, and he would not allow the existence of the animal to be disputed on board. He believed in it as certain good women believe in the leviathan—by faith, not by reason. The monster did exist, and he had sworn to rid the seas of it. He was a kind of Knight of Rhodes, going to meet the serpent which desolated the island. ●
Either Captain Farragut would kill the narwhal, or the narwhal would kill the captain. There was no third course.

The officers on board shared the opinion of their chief. They were ever chatting, discussing, and calculating the various chances of a meeting, watching narrowly the vast surface of the ocean. More than one took up his quarters voluntarily in the crosstrees, who would have cursed such a berth under any other circumstances. As long as the sun described its daily course, the rigging was crowded with sailors, whose feet were burned to such an extent by the heat of the deck as to render it unbearable; still the ●
Abraham Lincoln had not yet breasted the suspected waters of the Pacific. As to the ship's company, they desired nothing better than to meet the unicorn, to harpoon it, hoist it on board, and dispatch it. They watched the sea with eager attention.

Besides, Captain Farragut had spoken of a certain sum of two thousand dollars, set apart for whoever should first sight the monster, were he cabin boy, common seaman, or officer.

I leave you to judge how eyes were used on board the *Abraham Lincoln*.

For my own part, I was not behind the others, and left to no one my share ●
of daily observations. Only one among us, Conseil, seemed to protest by his indifference against the question which so interested us all, and seemed to be out of keeping with the general enthusiasm on board.

I have said that Captain Farragut had carefully provided his ship with every apparatus for catching the gigantic cetacean. No whaler had ever been better armed. We possessed every known engine, from the harpoon thrown by hand to the barbed arrows of the blunderbuss, and the explosive balls of the duck gun.

Recalling Facts

1. The narrator compared
   Captain Farragut to
   □ a. the leviathan.
   □ b. the Knight of Rhodes.
   □ c. Abraham Lincoln.

2. The officers on board
   □ a. shared their
        captain's feelings.
   □ b. disagreed with their
        captain's feelings.
   □ c. did not know their
        captain's feelings.

3. The name of the ship was the
   □ a. *Frigate.*
   □ b. *Abraham Lincoln.*
   □ c. *Conseil.*

4. The men expected to find the
   monster in the
   □ a. Indian Ocean.
   □ b. Atlantic Ocean.
   □ c. Pacific Ocean.

5. Whoever spotted the monster
   first would get a reward of
   □ a. $200.
   □ b. $1,000.
   □ c. $2,000.

Understanding the Passage

6. Captain Farragut was a
   man of great
   □ a. cruelty.
   □ b. indecision.
   □ c. determination.

7. The officers debated whether
   □ a. the monster existed.
   □ b. they would find the
        monster.
   □ c. the monster was worth
        the effort.

8. Taking up quarters in
   the crosstrees would
   ordinarily be
   □ a. eagerly sought.
   □ b. avoided.
   □ c. shared by the officers.

9. The narrator
   □ a. shared everyone's
        anticipation.
   □ b. showed indifference.
   □ c. wanted to go back
        to shore.

10. The ship was
    □ a. prepared for anything.
    □ b. overloaded with
         equipment.
    □ c. crowded with rigging.

If you ask your mother whether she knew about Peter Pan when she was a little girl she will say, "Why, of course, I did, child." If you ask her whether he rode on a goat in those days she will say, "What a foolish question to ask; certainly he did." Then if you ask your grandmother whether she knew about Peter Pan when she was a girl, she also says, "Why, of course, I did, child." But if you ask her whether he rode on a goat in those days, she says she never heard of his having a goat. Perhaps she has forgotten, just as she sometimes forgets your name and calls you Mildred, which is your mother's name. Still, she could hardly forget the goat. Therefore there was no goat when your grandmother was a little girl. This shows that, in telling the story of Peter Pan, to begin with the goat is as silly as to put on your jacket before your vest.

Of course, it also shows that Peter is ever so old, but he is really always the same age, so that does not matter in the least. His age is one week, and though he was born so long ago he has never had a birthday, nor is there the slightest chance of his ever having one. The reason is that he escaped from being a human when he was seven days old. He escaped by the window and flew back to Kensington Gardens.

If you think he was the only baby who ever wanted to escape, it shows how completely you have forgotten your own young days. When David heard this story first he was quite certain that he had never tried to escape, but I told him to think back hard, pressing his hands to his temples, and when he had done this hard, and even harder, he remembered a youthful desire to return to the treetops, and with that memory came others; that he had lain in bed planning to escape as soon as his mother was asleep, and how she had once caught him halfway up the chimney. All children could have such recollections if they would press their hands hard to their temples, for, having been birds before they were human, they are naturally a little wild during the first few weeks. So David tells me.

Recalling Facts

1. A mother would say she remembered Peter Pan riding a
   - ☐ a. goat.
   - ☐ b. mule.
   - ☐ c. horse.

2. Peter Pan's age was one
   - ☐ a. week.
   - ☐ b. month.
   - ☐ c. year.

3. Peter Pan escaped by the
   - ☐ a. cellar door.
   - ☐ b. skylight.
   - ☐ c. window.

4. David remembered an early desire to return to the
   - ☐ a. jungle.
   - ☐ b. nursery.
   - ☐ c. treetops.

5. The narrator claimed that before children become humans they are
   - ☐ a. clouds.
   - ☐ b. birds.
   - ☐ c. flowers.

Understanding the Passage

6. All three generations knew about
   - ☐ a. the goat.
   - ☐ b. Peter Pan.
   - ☐ c. the change in the story.

7. Peter Pan
   - ☐ a. worried about dying.
   - ☐ b. enjoyed his birthdays.
   - ☐ c. was immortal.

8. When David thought about his early days, he
   - ☐ a. began to regret his mistakes.
   - ☐ b. remembered a desire to escape.
   - ☐ c. was deeply embarrassed.

9. The narrator claims that the desire to escape is
   - ☐ a. unheard of among babies.
   - ☐ b. common among babies.
   - ☐ c. present only in older children.

10. Peter Pan was a
    - ☐ a. real boy.
    - ☐ b. magical being.
    - ☐ c. grandfather.

"Well, Zeena," Ethan ventured from the threshold. She did not move, and he continued: "Supper's about ready. Ain't you coming?"

She replied: "I don't feel as if I could touch a morsel."

It was the consecrated formula, and he expected it to be followed, as usual, by her rising and going down to supper. But she remained seated, and he could think of nothing more felicitous than: "I presume you're tired after the long ride."

Turning her head at this, she answered solemnly: "I'm a great deal sicker than you think." Her words fell on his ear with a strange shock of wonder. He had often heard her pronounce them before—what if at last they were true?

He advanced a step or two into the dim room. "I hope that's not so, Zeena," he said.

She continued to gaze at him through the twilight with a mien of wan authority, as of one consciously singled out for a great fate. "I've got complications," she said.

Ethan knew the word for one of exceptional import. Almost everybody in the neighborhood had "troubles," frankly localized and specified; but only the chosen had "complications." To have them was in itself a distinction, though it was also, in most cases, a death warrant. People struggled on for years with "troubles," but they almost always succumbed to "complications."

Ethan's heart was jerking to and fro between two extremities of feeling, but for the moment compassion prevailed. His wife looked so hard and lonely, sitting there in the darkness with such thoughts. "Is that what the new doctor told you?" he asked, instinctively lowering his voice.

"Yes. He says a regular doctor would want me to have an operation."

Ethan was aware that, in regard to the important question of surgical intervention, the female opinion of the neighborhood was divided, some glorying in the prestige conferred by operations while others shunned them as indelicate. Ethan, from motives of economy, had always been glad that Zeena was of the latter faction.

In the agitation caused by the gravity of her announcement he sought a consolatory short cut. "What do you know about this doctor anyway? Nobody ever told you that before." He saw his blunder before she could take it up: she wanted sympathy, not consolation.

"I didn't need to have anybody tell me I was losing ground every day. Everybody but you could see it."

Recalling Facts

1. Zeena complained that she had
   □ a. complications.
   □ b. troubles.
   □ c. illnesses.

2. Zeena was Ethan's
   □ a. mother.
   □ b. sister.
   □ c. wife.

3. The doctor Zeena saw was a
   □ a. regular doctor.
   □ b. new doctor.
   □ c. witch doctor.

4. A regular doctor would have insisted that Zeena
   □ a. have an operation.
   □ b. prepare her will.
   □ c. consult another physician for a second opinion.

5. Zeena wanted
   □ a. sympathy from Ethan.
   □ b. consolation from Ethan.
   □ c. money for an operation.

Understanding the Passage

6. When Ethan called Zeena for dinner, she was
   □ a. out riding.
   □ b. sitting down.
   □ c. in the living room.

7. People who had "complications" generally
   □ a. recovered.
   □ b. wanted a different doctor.
   □ c. died.

8. Ethan had
   □ a. mixed feelings about Zeena's problem.
   □ b. no compassion for Zeena.
   □ c. a fear of most doctors.

9. Women in the community did not agree on the merits of
   □ a. surgery.
   □ b. women doctors.
   □ c. marriage.

10. Zeena felt that
    □ a. her doctor had made a mistake.
    □ b. Ethan did not pay close attention to her.
    □ c. Ethan offered her too much sympathy.

from **The Prince and the Pauper** *by Mark Twain*

At each side of the gilded gate stood a living statue, that is to say, an erect and stately and motionless man-at-arms, clad in shining steel armor. At a respectful distance were many country folk, and people from the city, waiting for any chance glimpse of royalty. Splendid carriages were arriving and departing by several other noble gateways that pierced the royal enclosure.

Poor little Tom Canty in his rags approached, and was moving slowly and timidly past the sentinels, with a beating heart and arising hope, when all at once he caught sight through the golden bars of a spectacle that almost made him shout for joy. Within was a comely boy, tanned and brown with sturdy outdoor sports and exercises, whose clothing was all of lovely silks and satins, shining with jewels; at his hip a little jeweled sword and dagger; dainty buskins on his feet, with red heels; and on his head a jaunty crimson cap, with drooping plumes fastened with a great sparkling gem. Several gorgeous gentlemen stood near—his servants, without a doubt. Oh! He was a prince—a prince, a living prince, a real prince—without the shadow of a question, and the prayer of the pauper boy's heart was answered at last.

Tom's breath came quick and short with excitement, and his eyes grew big with wonder and delight. Everything gave way in his mind instantly to one desire: that was to get close to the prince, and have a good, devouring look at him. Before he knew what he was about, he had his face against the gate bars. The next instant one of the soldiers snatched him rudely away, and sent him spinning among the gaping crowd of country gawks and London idlers. The soldier said:

"Mind thy manners, thou young beggar!"

The crowd jeered and laughed, but the young prince sprang to the gate with his face flushed, and his eyes flashing with indignation, and cried out:

"How dare you use a poor lad like that! How dare you use the king my father's meanest subject so! Open the gates, and let him in!"

You should have seen that fickle crowd snatch off their hats then. You should have heard them cheer, and shout, "Long live the Prince of Wales!"

The soldiers presented arms with their halberds, opened the gates, and presented again as the little Prince of Poverty passed in.

Recalling Facts

1. The people were gathered to see
   - ☐ a. Tom Canty.
   - ☐ b. the prince.
   - ☐ c. the man-at-arms.

2. Tom Canty was dressed in
   - ☐ a. silks.
   - ☐ b. rags.
   - ☐ c. armor.

3. Tom Canty wanted to
   - ☐ a. get a closer look at the prince.
   - ☐ b. offer the prince a gift.
   - ☐ c. kick the soldier who grabbed him.

4. When the soldier shoved Tom away, the crowd
   - ☐ a. moaned.
   - ☐ b. hissed.
   - ☐ c. laughed.

5. The prince ordered his soldiers to
   - ☐ a. lead Tom out of the city.
   - ☐ b. give Tom a few coins.
   - ☐ c. let Tom inside the gate.

Understanding the Passage

6. Tom did not appear to be
   - ☐ a. curious.
   - ☐ b. jealous.
   - ☐ c. excited.

7. Tom could tell that the boy was a prince by his
   - ☐ a. clothes.
   - ☐ b. jewels.
   - ☐ c. both a and b.

8. The soldier who shoved Tom away did not think it would
   - ☐ a. upset the prince.
   - ☐ b. hurt Tom.
   - ☐ c. please the crowd.

9. The attitude of the crowd was
   - ☐ a. changeable.
   - ☐ b. inflexible.
   - ☐ c. restrained.

10. The prince treated Tom with
    - ☐ a. contempt.
    - ☐ b. kindness.
    - ☐ c. awe.

"Hepzibah, my beloved cousin, I am rejoiced!" exclaimed the Judge, most emphatically. "Now, at length, you have something to live for. Yes, and all of us, let me say, your friends and kindred, have more to live for than we had yesterday. I have lost no time in hastening to offer any assistance in my power towards making Clifford comfortable. He belongs to us all. I know how much he requires—how much he used to require—with his delicate taste, and his love of the beautiful. Anything in my house—pictures, books, wine, luxuries of the table—he may command them all! It would afford me most heartfelt gratification to see him! Shall I step in, this moment?"

"No," replied Hepzibah, her voice quivering too painfully to allow of many words. "He cannot see visitors!"

"A visitor, my dear cousin! Do you call me so?" cried the Judge, whose sensibility, it seems, was hurt by the coldness of the phrase. "Nay, then, let me be Clifford's host, and your own likewise. Come at once to my house. The country air, and all the conveniences—I may say luxuries—that I have gathered about me, will do wonders for him. And you and I, dear Hepzibah, will consult together, and watch together, and labor together, to make our dear Clifford happy. Come! Why should we make more words about what is both a duty and a pleasure on my part? Come to me at once!"

On hearing these so hospitable offers, and such generous recognition of the claims of kindred, Phoebe felt very much in the mood of running up to Judge Pyncheon, and giving him, of her own accord, the kiss from which she had so recently shrunk away. It was quite otherwise with Hepzibah; the Judge's smile seemed to operate on her acerbity of heart like sunshine upon vinegar, making it ten times sourer than ever.

"Clifford," said she, still too agitated to utter more than an abrupt sentence, "Clifford has a home here!"

"May Heaven forgive you, Hepzibah," said Judge Pyncheon, reverently lifting his eyes towards that high court of equity to which he appealed, "if you suffer any ancient prejudice or animosity to weigh with you in this matter! I stand here with an open heart, willing and anxious to receive yourself and Clifford into it. Do not refuse my good offices—my earnest propositions for your welfare!"

Recalling Facts

1. The Judge offered to give Clifford
   - ☐ a. a job.
   - ☐ b. some money.
   - ☐ c. a place to live.

2. Hepzibah said that Clifford could not
   - ☐ a. see visitors.
   - ☐ b. tolerate spicy foods.
   - ☐ c. pay his debts.

3. The Judge lived in the
   - ☐ a. city.
   - ☐ b. suburbs.
   - ☐ c. country.

4. Phoebe wanted to give the Judge
   - ☐ a. a hug.
   - ☐ b. a kiss.
   - ☐ c. some friendly advice.

5. The Judge's offer was
   - ☐ a. readily accepted by Hepzibah.
   - ☐ b. rejected by Hepzibah.
   - ☐ c. rejected by Clifford.

Understanding the Passage

6. The Judge appeared to be
   - ☐ a. unenthusiastic.
   - ☐ b. forgetful.
   - ☐ c. sincerely excited.

7. Clifford apparently had
   - ☐ a. a large fortune.
   - ☐ b. no friends.
   - ☐ c. special needs.

8. At this time, Clifford was living
   - ☐ a. with Hepzibah.
   - ☐ b. in a rest home.
   - ☐ c. by himself.

9. The Judge had recently tried to
   - ☐ a. kiss Phoebe.
   - ☐ b. sell his house.
   - ☐ c. lend Hepzibah money.

10. Hepzibah apparently did not
    - ☐ a. enjoy Clifford's company.
    - ☐ b. trust the Judge.
    - ☐ c. both a and b.

11 *from* The Christmas Tree and the Wedding *by Fyodor Dostoyevsky*

The other day I saw a wedding—but no! I would rather tell you about a Christmas tree. The wedding was superb. I liked it immensely. But the other incident was still finer. I don't know why it is that the sight of the wedding reminded me of the Christmas tree. This is the way it happened:

Exactly five years ago, on New Year's Eve, I was invited to a children's ball by a man high up in the business world, who had his connections, his circle of acquaintances, and his intrigues. So it seemed as though the children's ball was merely a pretext for the parents to come together and discuss matters of interest to themselves, quite innocently and casually.

I was an outsider, and, as I had no special matters to air, I was able to spend the evening independently of the others. There was another gentleman present who like myself had just stumbled upon this affair of domestic bliss. He was the first to attract my attention. His appearance was not that of a man of birth or high family. He was tall, rather thin, very serious, and well dressed. Apparently he had no heart for the family festivities. The instant he went off into a corner by himself the smile disappeared from his face, and his thick dark brows knitted into a frown. He knew no one except the host and showed every sign of being bored to death, though bravely sustaining the role of thorough enjoyment to the end. Later I learned that he was a provincial, had come to the capital on some important, brain-racking business, had brought a letter of recommendation to our host, and our host had taken him under his protection, not at all with love. It was merely out of politeness that he had invited him to the children's ball.

They did not play cards with him, they did not offer him cigars. No one entered into conversation with him. Possibly they recognized the bird by its feathers from a distance. Thus, my gentleman, not knowing what to do with his hands, was compelled to spend the evening stroking his whiskers. His whiskers were really fine, but he stroked them so assiduously that one got the feeling that the whiskers had come into the world first and afterwards the man in order to stroke them.

Recalling Facts

1. The narrator thought that the wedding was
   - ☐ a. boring.
   - ☐ b. superb.
   - ☐ c. phony.

2. At the children's ball, the narrator felt
   - ☐ a. like an observer.
   - ☐ b. nervous and ill at ease.
   - ☐ c. compelled to make small talk.

3. The tall gentleman was
   - ☐ a. a banker.
   - ☐ b. an intelligence agent.
   - ☐ c. a provincial.

4. At the ball, the tall gentleman
   - ☐ a. smoked cigars.
   - ☐ b. played cards.
   - ☐ c. neither a nor b.

5. The tall gentleman spent the evening
   - ☐ a. playing with children.
   - ☐ b. stroking his beard.
   - ☐ c. reading to himself.

Understanding the Passage

6. The narrator appeared to be
   - ☐ a. highly critical.
   - ☐ b. deeply suspicious.
   - ☐ c. quite curious.

7. The narrator felt the ball was held primarily for the benefit of
   - ☐ a. parents.
   - ☐ b. children.
   - ☐ c. unmarried women.

8. The narrator apparently was
   - ☐ a. a local businessman.
   - ☐ b. aware of the host's social standing.
   - ☐ c. related to the host.

9. The tall gentleman did not have
   - ☐ a. much fun at the ball.
   - ☐ b. the ability to smile.
   - ☐ c. both a and b.

10. The host felt obligated to
    - ☐ a. spend the evening entertaining the tall gentleman.
    - ☐ b. invite the tall gentleman to the ball.
    - ☐ c. introduce the narrator to all his friends.

We were down South, in Alabama—Bill Driscoll and myself—when this kidnapping idea struck us. It was, as Bill afterward expressed it, "during a moment of temporary mental apparition"; but we didn't find that out till later.

There was a town down there, as flat as a flannel cake, and called Summit, of course. It contained inhabitants of as undeleterious and self-satisfied a class of peasantry as ever clustered around a maypole.

Bill and me had a joint capital of about six hundred dollars, and we needed just two thousand dollars more to pull off a fradulent town lot scheme in Western Illinois with. We talked it over on the front steps of the hotel. Philoprogenitiveness, says we, is strong in semirural communities; therefore, and for other reasons, a kidnapping project ought to do better there than in the radius of newspapers that send reporters out in plain clothes to stir up talk about such things. We knew that Summit couldn't get after us with anything stronger than constables, and maybe some lackadaisical bloodhounds and a diatribe or two in the *Weekly Farmers' Budget*. So, it looked good.

We selected for our victim the only child of a prominent citizen named Ebenezer Dorset. The father was respectable and tight, a mortgage finan-cier and a stern, upright collection plate passer and forecloser. The kid was a boy of ten, with bas-relief freckles, and hair the color of the cover of the magazine you buy at the newsstand. Bill and me figured that Ebenezer would melt down for a ransom of two thousand dollars to a cent. But wait till I tell you.

About two miles from Summit was a little mountain, covered with a dense cedar bark. On the rear elevation of this mountain was a cave. There we stored provisions.

One evening after sundown, we drove in a buggy past old Dorset's house. The kid was in the street, throwing rocks at a kitten on the opposite fence.

"Hey, little boy!" says Bill, "would you like to have a bag of candy and a nice ride?"

The boy catches Bill neatly in the eye with a piece of brick.

"That will cost the old man an extra five hundred dollars," says Bill, climbing over the wheel.

That boy put up a fight like a welterweight cinnamon bear; but, at last, we got him down in the bottom of the buggy and drove away.

Recalling Facts

1. The kidnapping takes place in the town of
   - ☐ a. Alabama.
   - ☐ b. Summit.
   - ☐ c. Dorset.

2. The two men already had
   - ☐ a. $600.
   - ☐ b. $2,000.
   - ☐ c. $6,000.

3. Ebenezer Dorset had
   - ☐ a. several children.
   - ☐ b. one son.
   - ☐ c. no children.

4. The two men hid their provisions in a
   - ☐ a. hut.
   - ☐ b. mine shaft.
   - ☐ c. cave.

5. The two men took the boy away in a
   - ☐ a. car.
   - ☐ b. buggy.
   - ☐ c. wagon.

Understanding the Passage

6. Apparently the two men would soon
   - ☐ a. regret their decision to kidnap the boy.
   - ☐ b. collect their ransom.
   - ☐ c. turn themselves in to the police.

7. The town of Summit was
   - ☐ a. built on a mountain.
   - ☐ b. misnamed.
   - ☐ c. a lively, bustling place.

8. The two men needed the ransom to
   - ☐ a. pay back some old loans.
   - ☐ b. commit another crime.
   - ☐ c. buy their own news-paper business.

9. The town of Summit lacked a
   - ☐ a. church.
   - ☐ b. mortgage financier.
   - ☐ c. strong police force.

10. The kid
    - ☐ a. went peacefully with the two men.
    - ☐ b. put up a strong fight.
    - ☐ c. hated his stern father.

The night grew darker and darker; the stars seemed to sink deeper in the sky, and driving clouds occasionally hid them from his sight. He had never felt so lonely and dismal. He was, moreover, approaching the very place where many of the scenes of the ghost stories had been laid. In the center of the road stood an enormous tulip tree, which towered like a giant above all the other trees in the neighborhood. Its limbs were gnarled and fantastic, large enough to form trunks for ordinary trees, twisting down almost to the earth, and rising again into the air. It was connected with the tragical story of the unfortunate André, who had been taken prisoner hard by; and was universally known by the name of Major André's tree. People regarded it with a mixture of respect and superstition, partly out of sympathy for the fate of its ill-starred namesake and partly from the tales of strange sights and doleful lamentations told concerning it.

As Ichabod approached this fearful tree, he began to whistle; he thought his whistle was answered; it was but a blast sweeping sharply through the dry branches. As he approached a little nearer, he thought he saw something white hanging in the midst of the tree—he paused and ceased whistling; but on looking more narrowly, perceived that it was a place where the tree had been scathed by lightning, and the white wood laid bare. Suddenly he heard a groan—his teeth chattered, and his knees smote against the saddle; it was but the rubbing of one huge bough upon another, as they were swayed about by the breeze. He passed the tree in safety, but new perils lay before him.

About two hundred yards from the tree a small brook crossed the road, and ran into a marshy and thickly wooded glen, known by the name of Wiley's Swamp. A few rough logs, laid side by side, served for a bridge over this stream. On that side of the road where the brook entered the wood, a group of oaks and chestnuts, matted thick with wild grapevines, threw a cavernous gloom over it. To pass this bridge was the severest trial. It was here that the unfortunate André was captured, and under the cover of those chestnuts and vines were the sturdy yeomen concealed who surprised him. This has ever since been considered a haunted stream.

Recalling Facts

1. In the center of the road stood a
   - ☐ a. rosebush.
   - ☐ b. tulip tree.
   - ☐ c. stranger.

2. Major André was once
   - ☐ a. taken prisoner.
   - ☐ b. a famous war hero.
   - ☐ c. a well-known ghost story writer.

3. When Ichabod approached the tree, he began to
   - ☐ a. sing.
   - ☐ b. whistle.
   - ☐ c. pray.

4. The white thing that Ichabod saw in the tree was a
   - ☐ a. ghost.
   - ☐ b. shirt.
   - ☐ c. section of wood.

5. The stream that crossed the road was considered to be
   - ☐ a. polluted.
   - ☐ b. pleasant.
   - ☐ c. haunted.

Understanding the Passage

6. On the dark and lonely road, Ichabod began to
   - ☐ a. imagine things.
   - ☐ b. laugh hysterically.
   - ☐ c. tell himself ghost stories.

7. Ichabod was probably
   - ☐ a. walking.
   - ☐ b. riding a horse.
   - ☐ c. driving a wagon.

8. The night was
   - ☐ a. cool and dry.
   - ☐ b. windy.
   - ☐ c. extremely cold.

9. The bridge across the stream was
   - ☐ a. made of iron.
   - ☐ b. heavily traveled.
   - ☐ c. crudely buiilt.

10. The fate of Major André
    - ☐ a. was quickly forgotten.
    - ☐ b. was fondly remembered.
    - ☐ c. still troubled many people.

The youth saw that the ground in the deep shadows was cluttered with men, sprawling in every conceivable posture. Glancing narrowly into the more distant darkness, he caught occasional glimpses of visages that loomed pallid and ghostly, lit with a phosphorescent glow. These faces expressed in their lines the deep stupor of the tired soldiers. They made them appear like men drunk with wine. This bit of freedom might have appeared to an ethereal wanderer as a scene of the result of some frightful debauch.

On the other side of the fire the youth observed an officer asleep, seated bolt upright, with his back against a tree. There was something perilous in his position. Badgered by dreams, perhaps, he swayed with little bounces and starts, like an old, toddy-stricken grandfather in a chimney corner. Dust and stains were upon his face, and his lower jaw hung down as if lacking strength to assume its normal position. He was the picture of an exhausted soldier after a feast of war.

He had evidently gone to sleep with his sword in his arms. These two had slumbered in an embrace, but the weapon had been allowed in time to fall unheeded to the ground. The brass-mounted hilt lay in contact with some parts of the fire.

Within the gleam of rose and orange light from the burning sticks were other soldiers, snoring and heaving, or lying deathlike in slumber. A few pairs of legs were stuck forth, rigid and straight. The shoes displayed the mud or dust of marches and bits of rounded trousers, protruding from the blankets, showed rents and tears from hurried pitchings through the dense brambles.

The fire crackled musically. From it swelled light smoke. Overhead the foliage moved softly. The leaves, with their faces turned toward the blaze, were colored shifting hues of silver, often edged with red. Far off to the right, through a window in the forest, could be seen a handful of stars lying, like glittering pebbles, on the black level of the night.

Occasionally, in this low-arched hall, a soldier would arouse and turn his body to a new position, the experience of his sleep having taught him of uneven and objectionable places upon the ground under him. Or, perhaps, he would lift himself to a sitting posture, blink at the fire for an unintelligent moment, and then cuddle down again with a grunt of sleepy content.

Recalling Facts

1. The soldiers were sleeping
   - ☐ a. around a campfire.
   - ☐ b. on old, dirty cots.
   - ☐ c. in a farmer's field.

2. The officer who was sleeping sitting up had dropped his
   - ☐ a. gun.
   - ☐ b. cap.
   - ☐ c. sword.

3. The soldiers' boots were covered with
   - ☐ a. mud and dust.
   - ☐ b. blood.
   - ☐ c. leaves.

4. The leaves on the surrounding trees appeared to be
   - ☐ a. silver and red.
   - ☐ b. black as the night.
   - ☐ c. grey and lifeless.

5. All around the youth could see
   - ☐ a. deep shadows.
   - ☐ b. forest animals.
   - ☐ c. the enemy.

Understanding the Passage

6. The soldiers were
   - ☐ a. prisoners.
   - ☐ b. lying in ambush.
   - ☐ c. exhausted.

7. All the soldiers appeared to be
   - ☐ a. dirty.
   - ☐ b. young.
   - ☐ c. afraid.

8. This scene occurs
   - ☐ a. long after the war has ended.
   - ☐ b. during wartime.
   - ☐ c. in preparation for war.

9. As the soldiers slept, the youth
   - ☐ a. quietly observed them.
   - ☐ b. sketched them.
   - ☐ c. slipped away into the darkness.

10. Sleeping on the ground was
   - ☐ a. unbearable.
   - ☐ b. uncomfortable.
   - ☐ c. not allowed.

It was eleven o'clock that night when Mr. Pontellier returned from Klein's hotel. He was in an excellent humor, in high spirits, and very talkative. His entrance awoke his wife, who was in bed and fast asleep when he came in. He talked to her while he undressed, telling her anecdotes and bits of gossip that he had gathered during the day. From his trousers pockets he took a fistful of crumpled bank notes and a good deal of silver coin, which he piled on the bureau indiscriminately with keys, knife, handkerchief, and whatever else happened to be in his pockets. She was overcome with sleep, and answered him with little half utterances.

He considered it very discouraging that his wife, who was the sole object of his existence, evinced so little interest in things which concerned him, and valued so little his conversation.

Mr. Pontellier had forgotten the bonbons and peanuts for the boys. Notwithstanding he loved them very much, and went into the adjoining room where they slept to take a look at them and make sure that they were resting comfortably. The result of his investigation was far from satisfactory. He turned and shifted the youngsters about in bed. One of them began to kick and talk about a basket full of crabs.

Mr. Pontellier returned to his wife with the information that Raoul had a high fever and needed looking after. Then he lit a cigar and went and sat near the open door to smoke it.

Mrs. Pontellier was quite sure that Raoul had no fever. He had gone to bed perfectly well, she said, and nothing had ailed him all day. Mr. Pontellier was too well-acquainted with fever symptoms to be mistaken. He assured her the child was consuming at that moment in the next room.

He reproached his wife with her inattention, her habitual neglect of the children. If it was not a mother's place to look after children, whose on earth was it? He himself had his hands full with his brokerage business. He could not be in two places at once; making a living for his family on the street, and staying at home to see that no harm befell them. He talked in a monotonous, insistent way.

Mrs. Pontellier sprang out of bed and went into the next room. She soon came back and sat on the edge of the bed.

Recalling Facts

1. When Mr. Pontellier came home, he found his wife
   - ☐ a. dressing the children.
   - ☐ b. cleaning the attic.
   - ☐ c. asleep in bed.

2. From his pockets Mr. Pontellier took
   - ☐ a. a handful of coins.
   - ☐ b. several medicine bottles.
   - ☐ c. three cigars.

3. Mr. Pontellier forgot to bring the boys
   - ☐ a. a basket of crabs.
   - ☐ b. peanuts and bonbons.
   - ☐ c. new baseball mitts.

4. Mr. Pontellier believed that Raoul had
   - ☐ a. fallen out of bed.
   - ☐ b. been in a fight.
   - ☐ c. developed a fever.

5. Mr. Pontellier smoked his cigar
   - ☐ a. in bed.
   - ☐ b. by the fireplace.
   - ☐ c. near the open door.

Understanding the Passage

6. Mr. Pontellier wanted his wife to
   - ☐ a. listen to him when he talked.
   - ☐ b. prepare him a meal.
   - ☐ c. stop complaining about money.

7. Mr. Pontellier thought his wife was
   - ☐ a. discourteous.
   - ☐ b. uncaring.
   - ☐ c. deceiving.

8. Mrs. Pontellier did not believe that
   - ☐ a. Mr. Pontellier had been at Klein's hotel.
   - ☐ b. it was eleven o'clock.
   - ☐ c. Raoul had a fever.

9. Mr. Pontellier did not think he should have to
   - ☐ a. tend to the children.
   - ☐ b. work at the brokerage office.
   - ☐ c. bring his boys presents.

10. Mr. and Mrs. Pontellier did not seem to
   - ☐ a. disagree about anything.
   - ☐ b. be very happy with each other.
   - ☐ c. care about their children.

16 *from* Gulliver's Travels *by Jonathan Swift*

On the 17th we came in full view of a great island or continent (for we knew not whether) on the south side whereof was a small neck of land jutting out into the sea, and a creek too shallow to hold a ship of above one hundred tons. We cast anchor within a league of this creek. Our Captain sent a dozen of his men well armed in the longboat, with vessels for water if any could be found. I desired his leave to go with them, that I might see the country and make what discoveries I could. When we came to land we saw no river or spring, nor any sign of inhabitants. Our men therefore wandered on the shore to find out some fresh water near the sea, and I walked alone about a mile on the other side, where I observed the country all barren and rocky. I now began to be weary and seeing nothing to entertain my curiosity, I returned gently down towards the creek; and the sea being full in my view, I saw our men already got into the boat, and rowing for life to the ship. I was going to holler after them, although it had been to little purpose, when I observed a huge creature walking after them in the sea as fast as he could. He waded not much deeper than his knees and took prodigious strides, but our men had the start of him half a league, and the sea thereabouts being full of sharp-pointed rocks, the monster was not able to overtake the boat. This I was afterwards told, for I durst not stay to see the issue of that adventure; but ran as fast as I could the way I first went, and then climbed up a steep hill, which gave me some prospect of the country. I found it fully cultivated, but that which first surprised me was the length of the grass, which in those grounds that seemed to be kept for hay was about twenty feet high.

I fell into a high road, for so I took it to be, though it served to the inhabitants only as a footpath through a field of barley. Here I walked on for some time, but could see little on either side, it being now near harvest, and the corn rising at least forty feet.

Recalling Facts

1. The narrator wanted to
   - ☐ a. see the country.
   - ☐ b. stay with the Captain.
   - ☐ c. return home.

2. When they first landed, the men saw
   - ☐ a. many rivers and springs.
   - ☐ b. a dozen or so natives.
   - ☐ c. nothing in particular.

3. The men wandered along the shore searching for
   - ☐ a. native huts.
   - ☐ b. drinking water.
   - ☐ c. fresh food.

4. The men in the boat were being chased by what they thought was a
   - ☐ a. shark.
   - ☐ b. sea serpent.
   - ☐ c. monster.

5. The grass in this country was about
   - ☐ a. forty feet high.
   - ☐ b. twenty feet high.
   - ☐ c. ten feet high.

Understanding the Passage

6. The men in the longboat were
   - ☐ a. unwilling to go ashore.
   - ☐ b. prepared for trouble.
   - ☐ c. at war with the natives.

7. The narrator apparently
   - ☐ a. was curious about new places.
   - ☐ b. did not agree with the Captain.
   - ☐ c. had visited this country before.

8. As they headed away from land, the men seemed to be
   - ☐ a. unaware of the monster.
   - ☐ b. looking for the narrator.
   - ☐ c. badly frightened.

9. The natives of this country were
   - ☐ a. giants.
   - ☐ b. ordinary people.
   - ☐ c. midgets.

10. The natives of this country apparently worked as
    - ☐ a. fishermen.
    - ☐ b. farmers.
    - ☐ c. hunters.

Rosanna was the only new servant in our house. About four months before, my lady had been in London and had gone over to a reformatory, intended to save forlorn women from drifting back into bad ways, after they had got released from prison. The matron, seeing my lady took an interest in the place, pointed out a girl to her, named Rosanna Spearman, and told her a most miserable story. Rosanna Spearman had been a thief. The law laid hold of her, and the prison and the reformatory followed the lead of the law. The matron's opinion of Rosanna was that the girl was one in a thousand, and that she only wanted a chance to prove herself worthy of any Christian woman's interest in her. My lady (being a Christian woman, if ever there was one yet) said to the matron upon that, "Rosanna Spearman shall have her chance in my service." In a week afterward Rosanna Spearman entered this establishment as our second housemaid.

Not a soul was told the girl's story excepting Miss Rachel and me.

A fairer chance no girl could have had than was given to this poor girl. None of the other servants could cast her past life in her teeth, for none of the other servants knew what it had been. She had her wages and her privileges, like the rest of them, and every now and then a friendly word from my lady, in private, to encourage her. In return she showed herself well worthy of the kind treatment bestowed upon her. Though far from strong she went about her work modestly and uncomplainingly, doing it carefully and well. But somehow she failed to make friends among the other women servants, excepting my daughter Penelope, who was always kind to Rosanna, though never intimate with her.

I hardly know what the girl did to offend them. There was certainly no beauty about her to make the others envious; she was clearly the plainest woman in the house, with the additional misfortune of having one shoulder bigger than the other. What the servants chiefly resented, I think, was her silent tongue and her solitary ways. She read or worked in leisure hours when the rest gossiped. And when it came her turn to go out, nine times out of ten she quietly put on her bonnet, and had her turn by herself.

Recalling Facts

1. The story of Rosanna's past was told by
   - ☐ a. the police chief.
   - ☐ b. the matron.
   - ☐ c. Penelope.

2. Rosanna had been
   - ☐ a. a thief.
   - ☐ b. falsely accused.
   - ☐ c. a troublesome prisoner.

3. Rosanna was given the chance to work as a
   - ☐ a. waitress.
   - ☐ b. seamstress.
   - ☐ c. housemaid.

4. None of the other servants
   - ☐ a. knew Rosanna's story.
   - ☐ b. earned wages like Rosanna's.
   - ☐ c. had Rosanna's physical strength.

5. The plainest woman in the house was
   - ☐ a. Penelope.
   - ☐ b. Rosanna.
   - ☐ c. Miss Rachel.

Understanding the Passage

6. The matron of the reformatory thought Rosanna was
   - ☐ a. sneaky.
   - ☐ b. talkative.
   - ☐ c. special.

7. Rosanna had apparently had a
   - ☐ a. normal childhood.
   - ☐ b. tragic life.
   - ☐ c. tendency to be rude.

8. Rosanna appeared to be
   - ☐ a. appreciative.
   - ☐ b. resentful.
   - ☐ c. sociable.

9. The other women servants were
   - ☐ a. awed by Rosanna.
   - ☐ b. unimpressed by Rosanna.
   - ☐ c. intimidated by Rosanna.

10. The other women servants resented Rosanna's
   - ☐ a. beauty.
   - ☐ b. independence.
   - ☐ c. storytelling ability.

When young Mr. Schneidekoupon called upon Senator Ratcliffe to invite him to the dinner at Welckley's, he found that gentleman buried in work, as he averred, and very little disposed to converse. No! He did not now go out to dinner. In the present condition of the public business he found it impossible to spare the time for such amusements. He regretted to decline Mr. Schneidekoupon's offer, but there were imperative reasons why he should abstain for the present from social entertainments. He had made but one exception to his rule, and only at the pressing request of his old friend Senator Clinton, and on a very special occasion.

Mr. Schneidekoupon was deeply vexed—the more, he said, because he had meant to beg Mr. and Mrs. Clinton to be of the party, as well as a very charming lady who rarely went into society, but had almost consented to come.

"Who is that?" inquired the Senator.

"A Mrs. Lightfoot Lee, of New York. Probably you do not know her well enough to admire her as I do. But I think her quite the most intelligent woman I ever met."

The Senator's cold eyes rested for a moment on the young man's open face with a peculiar expression of distrust. Then he solemnly said, in his deepest tones:

"My young friend, at my time of life men have other things to occupy them than women, however intelligent they may be. Who else is to be of your party?"

Mr. Schneidekoupon named his list.

"And for Saturday evening at seven, did you say?"

"Saturday at seven."

"I fear there is little chance of my attending, but I will not absolutely decline. Perhaps when the moment arrives, I may find myself able to be there. But do not count upon me—no, do not count upon me. Good day, Mr. Schneidekoupon."

Schneidekoupon was rather a simpleminded young man. He saw no deeper than his neighbors into the secrets of the universe and he went off swearing roundly at "the infernal airs these senators give themselves." He told Mrs. Lee all the conversation, as indeed he was compelled to do under penalty of bringing her to his party under false pretenses.

"Just my luck," said he; "here I am asking no end of people to meet a man, who at the same time says he shall probably not come."

Recalling Facts

1. Mr. Schneidekoupon called on Senator Ratcliffe to invite him
   - ☐ a. over for tea.
   - ☐ b. to a Christmas party.
   - ☐ c. to dinner.

2. When Mr. Schneidekoupon arrived, Senator Ratcliffe was
   - ☐ a. sleeping.
   - ☐ b. busy working.
   - ☐ c. picking flowers.

3. Mrs. Lightfoot Lee was from
   - ☐ a. New York.
   - ☐ b. New England.
   - ☐ c. New Jersey.

4. The invitation was for
   - ☐ a. Friday at nine.
   - ☐ b. Saturday at seven.
   - ☐ c. Sunday at five.

5. Mr. Schneidekoupon was
   - ☐ a. a Senator.
   - ☐ b. an influential intellectual.
   - ☐ c. not very bright.

Understanding the Passage

6. Senator Ratcliffe had
   - ☐ a. very little spare time.
   - ☐ b. few friends.
   - ☐ c. a dislike for Mrs. Lee.

7. Senator Ratcliffe's refusal to commit to the dinner party
   - ☐ a. put Mr. Schneidekoupon in a difficult spot.
   - ☐ b. forced the cancellation of the party.
   - ☐ c. was warmly appreciated by Mrs. Lee.

8. Senator Clinton and Senator Ratcliffe appeared to be
   - ☐ a. good friends.
   - ☐ b. political enemies.
   - ☐ c. very different personalities.

9. Senator Ratcliffe was not impressed by
   - ☐ a. Mr. Schneidekoupon's initial invitation.
   - ☐ b. the location of the planned party.
   - ☐ c. both a and b.

10. Mr. Schneidekoupon was
    - ☐ a. annoyed with Senator Ratcliffe.
    - ☐ b. in love with Mrs. Lightfoot Lee.
    - ☐ c. unable to decide on a time for his dinner party.

from **Sherlock Holmes and The Hound of the Baskervilles** *by Arthur Conan Doyle*

Sir Charles Baskerville was in the habit every night before going to bed of walking down the famous yew alley of Baskerville Hall. The evidence of the Barrymores shows that this had been his custom. On the fourth of May Sir Charles had declared his intention of starting next day for London, and had ordered Barrymore to prepare his luggage. That night he went out as usual for his nocturnal walk, in the course of which he was in the habit of smoking a cigar. He never returned. At twelve o'clock Barrymore, finding the hall door still open, became alarmed. Lighting a lantern, he went in search of his master. The day had been wet, and Sir Charles's footmarks were easily traced down the alley. Halfway down this walk there is a gate which leads out on to the moor. There were indications that Sir Charles had stood for some little time here. He then proceeded down the alley, and it was at the far end of it that his body was discovered. One fact which has not been explained is the statement of Barrymore that his master's footprints altered their character from the time that he passed the moor gate, and that he appeared from thence onward to have been walking upon his toes. One Murphy, a gypsy horse dealer, was on the moor at no great distance at the time, but he appears by his own confession to have been the worse for drink. He declares that he heard cries but is unable to state from what direction they came. No signs of violence were to be discovered upon Sir Charles's person. The doctor's evidence pointed to an almost incredible facial distortion—so great that Dr. Mortimer refused at first to believe that it was indeed his friend and patient who lay before him—but it was explained that that is a symptom which is not unusual in cases of dyspnea and death from cardiac exhaustion. This explanation was borne out by the postmortem examination, which showed long-standing organic disease. The coroner's jury returned a verdict in accordance with the medical evidence. It is well that this is so, for it is obviously of the utmost importance that Sir Charles's heir should settle at the Hall and continue the good work which has been so sadly interrupted. It is understood that the next of kin is Mr. Henry Baskerville.

Recalling Facts

1. Sir Charles planned to visit
   - ☐ a. London.
   - ☐ b. Manchester.
   - ☐ c. Baskerville Square.

2. Every night Sir Charles
   - ☐ a. took a walk.
   - ☐ b. smoked a cigar.
   - ☐ c. both a and b.

3. Barrymore became alarmed about Sir Charles around
   - ☐ a. 8 P.M.
   - ☐ b. 10 P.M.
   - ☐ c. midnight.

4. Murphy was a
   - ☐ a. doctor.
   - ☐ b. horse dealer.
   - ☐ c. police officer.

5. Sir Charles apparently died from
   - ☐ a. a knife wound.
   - ☐ b. cardiac exhaustion.
   - ☐ c. a brain hemorrhage.

Understanding the Passage

6. Sir Charles appeared to be a man of
   - ☐ a. unstable emotions.
   - ☐ b. steady habits.
   - ☐ c. great suspicions.

7. The alley of Baskerville Hall was probably
   - ☐ a. a brick path.
   - ☐ b. a dirt path.
   - ☐ c. paved with asphalt.

8. The changed footprints were
   - ☐ a. not that unusual.
   - ☐ b. apparently made by a horse.
   - ☐ c. mysterious.

9. Murphy made a poor witness because he was
   - ☐ a. hard of hearing.
   - ☐ b. not well educated.
   - ☐ c. drunk.

10. Apparently, Sir Charles had
   - ☐ a. many enemies.
   - ☐ b. no heirs.
   - ☐ c. been sick for a long time.

from **Captains Courageous** *by Rudyard Kipling*

They made berth after berth to the northward, the dories out almost every day, running along the east edge of the Grand Bank in thirty- to forty-fathom water, and fishing steadily.

It was here Harvey first met the squid, who is one of the best cod baits, but uncertain in his moods. They were waked out of their bunks one black night by yells of "Squid O!" from Salters, and for an hour and a half every soul aboard hung over his squid jig—a piece of lead painted red and armed at the lower end with a circle of pins bent backward like half-opened ●umbrella ribs. The squid—for some unknown reason—likes, and wraps himself round, this thing. He is then hauled up before he can escape from the pins. But as he leaves his home he squirts first water and next ink into his captor's face, and it was curious to see the men weaving their heads from side to side to dodge the shot. They were as black as sweeps when the flurry ended, but a pile of fresh squid lay on the deck, and the large cod thinks very well of a little shiny piece of squid tentacle at the tip of ● a clam-baited hook. Next day they caught many fish, and met the *Carrie Pitman*, to whom they shouted their luck, and she wanted to trade—seven cod for one fair-sized squid; but Disko would not agree at the price, and the *Carrie* dropped sullenly to leeward and anchored half a mile away, in the hope of striking on to some for herself.

Disko said nothing till after supper, when he sent Dan and Manuel out to buoy the *We're Here's* cable and announced his intention of turning in with the broadaxe. Dan naturally repeated these remarks to a dory from ● the *Carrie*, who wanted to know why they were buoying their cable, since their were not on rocky bottom.

"Dad sez he wouldn't trust a ferryboat within five mile o' you," Dan howled cheerfully.

"Why don't he git out, then? Who's hinderin'?" said the other.

" 'Cause you've jest the same as lee-bowed him, an' he don't take that from any boat, not to speak o' sech a driftin' gurry-butt as you be."

"She ain't driftin' any this trip," said the man angrily, for the *Carrie Pitman* had an unsavory reputation for breaking her ground tackle.

Recalling Facts

1. The dories operated in the
   □ a. East Bank.
   □ b. Grand Canal.
   □ c. Grand Bank.

2. "Squid O!" was yelled by
   □ a. Harvey.
   □ b. Salters.
   □ c. Disko.

3. The squid shot
   □ a. water only.
   □ b. ink only.
   □ c. water and ink.

4. The *Carrie Pitman* wanted
   to trade
   □ a. cod for squid.
   □ b. squid for clams.
   □ c. clams for squid and cod.

5. Dan and Manuel
   □ a. were members of the
      Carrie Pitman crew.
   □ b. buoyed their cable.
   □ c. spent the night with a
      broadaxe.

Understanding the Passage

6. Squid were caught
   □ a. to be used as bait.
   □ b. for their ink.
   □ c. as food for the crew.

7. The sailors became
   black from
   □ a. the dirt on board
      the ship.
   □ b. cleaning cod.
   □ c. the squid's ink.

8. A squid was
   □ a. relatively worthless.
   □ b. worth more than
      several cod.
   □ c. extremely easy to catch.

9. Disko appeared to be
   □ a. a trusting man.
   □ b. a suspicious man.
   □ c. an incompetent sailor.

10. Apparently, the
    Carrie Pitman
    □ a. was much larger than
       the *We're Here.*
    □ b. had its own supply
       of squid.
    □ c. had frequent trouble
       with its ground tackle.

21 *from* Narrative of the Life of Frederick Douglass *by Frederick Douglass*

I was born in Tuckahoe, near Hillsborough, and about twelve miles from Easton, in Talbot County, Maryland. I have no accurate knowledge of my age, never having seen any authentic record containing it. By far the larger part of the slaves know as little of their age as horses know of theirs, and it is the wish of most masters within my knowledge to keep their slaves thus ignorant. I do not remember to have ever met a slave who could tell of his birthday. They seldom come nearer to it than planting time, harvesting, cherry time, springtime, or falltime. A lack of information concerning my own was a source of unhappiness to me even during childhood. The white children could tell their ages. I could not tell why I ought to be deprived of the same privilege. I was not allowed to make any inquiries of my master concerning it. He deemed all such inquiries on the part of a slave improper and impertinent, and evidence of a restless spirit. The nearest estimate I can give makes me now between twenty-seven and twenty-eight years of age. I come to this, from hearing my master say, sometime during 1835, I was about seventeen years old.

My mother was named Harriet Bailey. She was the daughter of Isaac and Betsey Bailey, both colored, and quite dark. My mother was of a darker complexion than either my grandmother or grandfather.

My father was a white man. He was admitted to be such by all I ever heard speak of my parentage. The opinion was also whispered that my master was my father; but of the correctness of this opinion, I know nothing; the means of knowing was withheld from me. My mother and I were separated when I was but an infant—before I knew her as my mother. It is a common custom, in the part of Maryland from which I ran away, to part children from their mothers at a very early age. Frequently, before the child has reached its twelfth month, its mother is taken from it, and hired out on some farm a considerable distance off, and the child is placed under the care of an old woman, too old for field labor. For what this separation is done, I do not know, unless it be to hinder the development of the child's affection toward its mother.

Recalling Facts

1. The narrator did not know
   - ☐ a. where he was born.
   - ☐ b. his birthday.
   - ☐ c. the name of his mother.

2. The narrator estimated that he was about
   - ☐ a. twenty-one years old.
   - ☐ b. twenty-four years old.
   - ☐ c. twenty-seven years old.

3. The narrator's father was probably a
   - ☐ a. free white.
   - ☐ b. slave.
   - ☐ c. free black.

4. The narrator and his mother were
   - ☐ a. very close.
   - ☐ b. separated early.
   - ☐ c. sold together.

5. The narrator had grown up in
   - ☐ a. Virginia.
   - ☐ b. Maryland.
   - ☐ c. Delaware.

Understanding the Passage

6. Slaves often
   - ☐ a. marked their birthdays by the season.
   - ☐ b. had their own birth certificates.
   - ☐ c. didn't care how old they were.

7. The narrator's mother and father were
   - ☐ a. deeply in love.
   - ☐ b. not married.
   - ☐ c. both dead.

8. The narrator had not spent much time with
   - ☐ a. his mother.
   - ☐ b. his father.
   - ☐ c. both a and b.

9. Slaveowners treated their slaves
   - ☐ a. with great love.
   - ☐ b. with little compassion.
   - ☐ c. like family members.

10. The narrator was apparently raised by
    - ☐ a. his master.
    - ☐ b. an old female slave.
    - ☐ c. his mother's parents.

22 *from* **Heart of Darkness** *by Joseph Conrad*

Going up that river was like traveling back to the earliest beginnings of the world, when vegetation rioted on the earth and the big trees were kings. An empty stream, a great silence, and an impenetrable forest. The air was warm, thick, heavy, sluggish. There was no joy in the brilliance of sunshine. The long stretches of the waterway ran on, deserted, into the gloom of overshadowed distances. On silvery sandbanks hippos and alligators sunned themselves side by side. The broadening waters flowed through a mob of wooded islands; you lost your way on that river as you would in a desert, and butted all day long against shoals, trying to find the channel, till you thought yourself bewitched and cut off forever from everything you had known once—somewhere—far away—in another existence perhaps. There were moments when one's past came back to one, as it will sometimes when you have not a moment to spare to yourself; but it came in the shape of an unrestful and noisy dream, remembered with wonder amongst the overwhelming realities of this strange world of plants, and water, and silence. And this stillness of life did not in the least resemble a peace. It was the stillness of an implacable force brooding over an inscrutable intention. It looked at you with a vengeful aspect. I got used to it afterwards; I did not see it any more; I had no time. I had to keep guessing at the channel; I had to discern, mostly by inspiration, the signs of hidden banks; I watched for sunken stones; I was learning to clap my teeth smartly before my heart flew out, when I shaved by a fluke some infernal sly old snag that would have ripped the life out of the tin-pot steamboat and drowned all the pilgrims; I had to keep a lookout for the signs of dead wood we could cut up in the night for next day's steaming. When you have to attend to things of that sort, to the mere incidents of the surface, the reality—the reality, I tell you—fades. The inner truth is hidden—luckily, luckily. But I felt it all the same; I felt often its mysterious stillness watching me at my monkey tricks. I managed not to sink that steamboat on my first trip. It's a wonder to me yet.

Recalling Facts

1. The river mentioned in the passage was surrounded by
   □ a. fertile farmland.
   □ b. wilderness.
   □ c. a growing city.

2. The speaker was struck by the
   □ a. loud noises all around him.
   □ b. mysterious stillness of the area.
   □ c. large number of boats on the river.

3. During the journey, the speaker looked for
   □ a. dead wood.
   □ b. hostile natives.
   □ c. both a and b.

4. The speaker was traveling in a
   □ a. rowboat.
   □ b. riverboat.
   □ c. steamboat.

5. On his first trip up the river, the speaker
   □ a. felt confident of success.
   □ b. managed not to sink the boat.
   □ c. became very sick.

Understanding the Passage

6. The speaker was apparently
   □ a. piloting the boat.
   □ b. the only person on the boat.
   □ c. very familiar with the area.

7. The speaker found his journey to be
   □ a. disappointing.
   □ b. difficult.
   □ c. short-lived.

8. The river was filled with
   □ a. poisonous snakes.
   □ b. polluted water.
   □ c. obstacles.

9. The speaker felt lucky to have
   □ a. completed his journey successfully.
   □ b. been chosen for the trip.
   □ c. seen alligators and hippos.

10. During his journey, the speaker felt
    □ a. isolated from the rest of the world.
    □ b. lonely for his family.
    □ c. grateful for the peaceful stillness.

from **The Countess of Rudolstadt** *by George Sand*

Cagliostro asked, on entering his magical laboratory with me, if I would consent to be blindfolded and to follow him holding his hand. As I knew him to be a man of good reputation, I did not hesitate to accept his offer. I only made it a condition that he should not leave me for an instant. "I was about," said he, "to beseech you not to withdraw from me a single step, and not to let go my hand, whatever may happen, whatever emotion you may experience." I promised this, but a simple affirmation was not suf- ● ficient. He made me solemnly swear that I would not make a gesture nor an exclamation; in short, that I would remain mute and impassive. Then he put on his glove, and, after having covered my head with a hood of black velvet which fell as low as my shoulder, he made me walk about five minutes without hearing any door open or shut. The hood prevented my perceiving any change in the atmosphere. I therefore could not know if I had left the laboratory, so many turnings and windings did he make me take in order to deprive me of all knowledge of the direction we were ● pursuing. Finally he stopped, and took off the hood so lightly that I did not perceive it. My breathing becoming more free, alone informed me that I had the liberty of looking, but I was in such thick darkness that I was not much better informed. Little by little, nevertheless, I saw a luminous star, at first vacillating and feeble, but soon clear and brilliant, displayed before me. At first, it seemed very far off. Then, when it reached its full brightness, it appeared to me quite near. That was the effect, I think, of a light more ● or less intense behind a transparency. Cagliostro made me approach this star, which was a hole pierced in the wall. On the other side of that wall, I saw a strangely decorated chamber, filled with candles placed in a symmetrical order. That apartment had, in its ornaments and arrangement, all the appearance of a place intended for magical operations. But I had no time to examine it much. My attention was engrossed by a person seated before a table. He was alone and had his face hidden in his hands as if plunged in deep meditation.

Recalling Facts

1. The speaker agreed to be
   - ☐ a. blindfolded.
   - ☐ b. left alone.
   - ☐ c. both a and b.

2. The speaker solemnly swore to
   - ☐ a. tell others about the laboratory.
   - ☐ b. remain completely silent.
   - ☐ c. speak only when spoken to.

3. Cagliostro led the speaker on a walk that lasted
   - ☐ a. thirty seconds.
   - ☐ b. five minutes.
   - ☐ c. forty minutes.

4. After the hood was removed, the speaker saw a
   - ☐ a. door.
   - ☐ b. window.
   - ☐ c. star.

5. The face of the man seated at the table was
   - ☐ a. scarred.
   - ☐ b. hidden.
   - ☐ c. uncovered.

Understanding the Passage

6. The speaker appeared to be
   - ☐ a. very suspicious.
   - ☐ b. overly nervous.
   - ☐ c. quite trusting.

7. To Cagliostro, the speaker's cooperation was
   - ☐ a. absolutely essential.
   - ☐ b. important, but not vital.
   - ☐ c. not at all necessary.

8. Cagliostro used the hood to
   - ☐ a. hurt the speaker.
   - ☐ b. disorient the speaker.
   - ☐ c. trap the speaker.

9. When the hood was removed, the speaker thought the room was
   - ☐ a. very dark.
   - ☐ b. filled with luminous stars.
   - ☐ c. very small.

10. The speaker apparently did not know
    - ☐ a. what was going to happen next.
    - ☐ b. Cagliostro's real name.
    - ☐ c. if the candles were really lit.

from **Peter Pan in Kensington Gardens** *by James M. Barrie*

The birds on the island never got used to Peter. His oddities tickled them every day, as if they were quite new, though it was really the birds that were new. They came out of the eggs daily, and laughed at him at once; then off they soon flew, and other birds came out of other eggs; and so it went on forever. The crafty mother birds, when they tired of sitting on their eggs, used to get the young ones to break their shells a day before the right time by whispering to them that now was their chance to see Peter washing or drinking or eating. Thousands gathered round him daily to watch him do these things, just as you watch the peacocks, and they screamed with delight when he lifted the crusts they flung him with his hands instead of in the usual way with the mouth. All this food was brought to him from the Gardens by the birds. He would not eat worms or insects (which they thought very silly of him), so they brought him bread in their beaks. Thus, when you cry out, "Greedy! Greedy!" to the bird that flies away with the big crust, you know now that you ought not to do this, for he is very likely taking it to Peter Pan.

Peter wore no nightgown now. You see, the birds were always begging him for bits of it to line their nests with, and, being very good-natured, he could not refuse, so he had hidden what was left of it. But, though he was now quite naked, you must not think that he was cold or unhappy. He was usually very happy, and the reason was that Solomon had kept his promise and taught him many of the bird ways. To be easily pleased, for instance, and always to be really doing something, and to think that whatever he was doing was a thing of vast importance. Peter became very clever at helping the birds to build their nests; soon he could build better than a wood pigeon, and nearly as well as a blackbird, though never did he satisfy the finches, and he made nice little water troughs near the nests and dug up worms for the young ones with his fingers. He also became very learned in bird lore, and knew an east wind from a west wind by its smell.

*Reading Time*_____ *Comprehension Score*_____ *Words per Minute*_____ 61

Recalling Facts

1. Mother birds got their young
   ones to break their shells
   early by
   □ a. sitting on them.
   □ b. telling them about Peter.
   □ c. dropping the eggs.

2. Peter's food came from the
   □ a. Gardens.
   □ b. Restaurant.
   □ c. Park.

3. Peter refused to eat
   □ a. snails.
   □ b. carrots.
   □ c. insects.

4. The birds lined their nests
   with bits of Peter's
   □ a. nightgown.
   □ b. pants.
   □ c. shirt.

5. Peter learned to tell wind
   direction by
   □ a. holding his finger
       in the air.
   □ b. smelling it.
   □ c. watching the birds.

Understanding the Passage

6. The birds found Peter to be
   □ a. boring.
   □ b. mildly amusing.
   □ c. endlessly fascinating.

7. Peter picked up his food
   with his
   □ a. mouth.
   □ b. hands.
   □ c. feet.

8. Peter's diet consisted
   mostly of
   □ a. meat.
   □ b. vegetables.
   □ c. bread.

9. Solomon appears to
   be Peter's
   □ a. teacher.
   □ b. archenemy.
   □ c. younger brother.

10. The hardest birds to please
    were the
    □ a. wood pigeons.
    □ b. blackbirds.
    □ c. finches.

Piotr Ivanovitch continued to fix his eyes on the copy of the *Vyedomosti* which had just been handed to him.

"Gentlemen!" said he, "so Ivan Ilyitch is dead!"

"You don't say so!"

"Here! Read for yourself," said he to Feodor Vasilyevitch, handing him the paper, which had not yet lost its odor of freshness.

Heavy black lines enclosed these printed words: "Praskovia Feodorovna Golovina, with heartfelt sorrow, announces to relatives and friends the death of her beloved husband, Ivan Ilyitch Golovin, member of the Court of Appeals, who departed this life on February 16, 1882. The funeral will take place on Friday, at one o'clock in the afternoon."

Ivan Ilyitch had been the colleague of the gentlemen there assembled, and all liked him. He had been ill for several weeks, and it was said that his case was incurable. His place was kept vacant for him; but it had been decided, that, in case of his death, Aleksyeef might be assigned to his place, while either Vinnikof or Shtabel would take Aleskyeef's place. And so, on hearing of Ivan Ilyitch's death, the first thought of each of the gentlemen gathered in the cabinet was in regard to the changes and promotions which might be brought about, among the members of the council and their acquaintances, in consequence of this death.

"Now, surely, I shall get either Shtabel's or Vinnikof's place," was Feodor Vasilyevitch's thought. "It has been promised me for a long time; and this promotion will mean an increase in my salary of eight hundred rubles, not to mention allowances."

"I must propose right away to have my brother-in-law transferred from Kaluga," thought Piotr Ivanovitch. "My wife will be very glad. Now it will be impossible for her to say that I have never done anything for her relations."

"I have been thinking that he wouldn't get up again," said Piotr Ivanovitch aloud. "It is too bad."

"But what was the matter with him?"

"The doctors could not determine. That is to say, they determined it, but each in his own way. When I saw him the last time, it seemed to me that he was getting better. But I haven't been to see him since the Christmas holidays. I kept meaning to go."

"Did he have any property?"

"His wife had a little, I think. But a mere pittance."

"Well, we must go to see her."

Recalling Facts

1. The *Vyedomosti* was
   - ☐ a. a funeral director.
   - ☐ b. a newspaper.
   - ☐ c. the Court of Appeals.

2. Praskovia was the first name of Ivan Ilyitch's
   - ☐ a. wife.
   - ☐ b. daughter.
   - ☐ c. mother.

3. Ivan died in
   - ☐ a. February of 1782.
   - ☐ b. November of 1888.
   - ☐ c. February of 1882.

4. Ivan's place on the Court of Appeals was to be filled by
   - ☐ a. Aleksyeef.
   - ☐ b. Shtabel.
   - ☐ c. Vinnikof.

5. Feodor Vasilyevitch hoped to get a raise of
   - ☐ a. 800 dollars.
   - ☐ b. 800 rubles.
   - ☐ c. 8,000 rubles.

Understanding the Passage

6. The gentlemen were
   - ☐ a. colleagues of Ivan.
   - ☐ b. relatives of Ivan.
   - ☐ c. medical professionals.

7. Ivan's case had been considered
   - ☐ a. mild.
   - ☐ b. terminal.
   - ☐ c. serious, but not life-threatening.

8. The gentlemen's first concern was for
   - ☐ a. Ivan's family.
   - ☐ b. their relatives.
   - ☐ c. their own futures.

9. Apparently, promotions were
   - ☐ a. made automatically every six months.
   - ☐ b. based on performance.
   - ☐ c. made when a seat fell vacant.

10. The doctors
    - ☐ a. agreed on the cause of death.
    - ☐ b. did not think Ivan was really sick.
    - ☐ c. disagreed on what killed Ivan.

King Solomon, who was so wise that he had power over evil such as no man has had before or since, set himself to work to put those enemies of mankind out of the way. Some he conjured into bottles, and sank into the depth of the sea; some he buried in the earth; some he destroyed altogether, as one burns hair in a candle flame.

Now, one pleasant day when King Solomon was walking in his garden with his hands behind his back, and his thoughts busy as bees with this or that, he came face to face with a Demon, who was a prince of his kind. "Ho, little man!" cried the evil spirit, in a loud voice, "art not thou the wise King Solomon who conjured my brethren into brass chests and glass bottles? Come, try a fall at wrestling with me, and whoever conquers shall be master over the other for all time. What do you say to such an offer as that?"

"I say aye!" said King Solomon, and, without another word, he stripped off his royal robes and stood bare breasted, man to man with the other.

The world never saw the like of that wrestling match betwixt the king and the Demon, for they struggled and strove together from the seventh hour in the morning to the sunset in the evening, and during that time the sky was clouded over as black as night, and the lightning forked and shot, and the thunder roared and bellowed, and the earth shook and quaked.

But at last the king gave the enemy an undertwist, and flung him down on the earth so hard that the apples fell from the trees; and then, panting and straining, he held the evil one down, knee on neck. Thereupon the sky presently cleared again, and all was as pleasant as a spring day.

King Solomon bound the Demon with spells, and made him serve him for seven years. First, he had him build a splendid palace, the like of which was not to be seen within the bounds of the seven rivers; then he made him set around the palace a garden, such as I for one wish I may see sometime or other. Then, when the Demon had done all that the king wished, the king conjured him into a bottle, corked it tightly, and set the royal seal on the stopper.

Recalling Facts

1. Solomon came face to face
   with a Demon while he was
   - [ ] a. hunting.
   - [ ] b. gardening.
   - [ ] c. walking.

2. The Demon challenged
   Solomon to a
   - [ ] a. wrestling match.
   - [ ] b. duel.
   - [ ] c. fistfight.

3. The struggle between
   Solomon and the Demon
   lasted
   - [ ] a. seven minutes.
   - [ ] b. most of a day.
   - [ ] c. nearly a week.

4. During the bout, the sky
   - [ ] a. stayed bright and sunny.
   - [ ] b. was grey and dismal.
   - [ ] c. turned black as night.

5. Solomon made the Demon
   serve him for
   - [ ] a. one year.
   - [ ] b. five years.
   - [ ] c. seven years.

Understanding the Passage

6. King Solomon wanted to
   - [ ] a. eliminate evil.
   - [ ] b. destroy the world.
   - [ ] c. put Demons to work.

7. The Demon
   - [ ] a. possessed ordinary
     powers.
   - [ ] b. was a fair match
     for Solomon.
   - [ ] c. was only having a
     little fun.

8. The fight between Solomon
   and the Demon was
   - [ ] a. earthshaking and
     unprecedented.
   - [ ] b. typical of events of
     this time.
   - [ ] c. stopped when the
     king was hurt.

9. The fight had a direct
   impact on
   - [ ] a. other kings.
   - [ ] b. trees and rivers.
   - [ ] c. the weather.

10. Solomon turned the
    Demon into a
    - [ ] a. good person.
    - [ ] b. personal slave.
    - [ ] c. stone pillar.

It was a small party, got up rather in a hurry by Lady Narborough, who was a very clever woman, with what Lord Henry used to describe as the remains of really remarkable ugliness. She had proved an excellent wife to one of our most tedious ambassadors, and having buried her husband properly in a marble mausoleum, which she had herself designed, and married off her daughters to some rich, rather elderly men, she devoted herself now to the pleasures of French fiction, French cookery, and French *esprit* when she could get it.

Dorian was one of her special favorites, and she always told him that she was extremely glad she had not met him in early life. "I know, my dear, I should have fallen madly in love with you," she used to say, "and thrown my bonnet right over the mills for your sake. It is most fortunate that you were not thought of at the time. As it was, our bonnets were so unbecoming, and the mills were so occupied in trying to raise the wind, that I never had even a flirtation with anybody. However, that was all Narborough's fault. He was dreadfully shortsighted, and there is no pleasure in taking in a husband who never sees anything."

Her guests this evening were rather tedious. The fact was, as she explained to Dorian, behind a very shabby fan, one of her married daughters had come up quite suddenly to stay with her, and, to make matters worse, had actually brought her husband with her. "I think it is most unkind of her, my dear," she whispered. "Of course I go and stay with them every summer after I come from Homburg, but then an old woman like me must have fresh air sometimes, and besides, I really wake them up. You don't know what an existence they lead down there. It is pure unadulterated country life. They get up early, because they have so much to do, and go to bed early because they have so little to think about. There has not been a scandal in the neighborhood since the time of Queen Elizabeth, and consequently they all fall asleep after dinner. You shan't sit next to either of them. You shall sit by me, and amuse me."

Dorian murmured a graceful compliment, and looked round the room. Yes: it was certainly a tedious party.

Recalling Facts

1. The party was being given by
   - ☐ a. Lord Henry.
   - ☐ b. Lady Narborough.
   - ☐ c. Lord Narborough.

2. Lady Narborough enjoyed reading
   - ☐ a. French fiction.
   - ☐ b. Russian poetry.
   - ☐ c. English novels.

3. Lady Narborough's daughters were all
   - ☐ a. living with her.
   - ☐ b. married to rather elderly men.
   - ☐ c. traveling to Homburg.

4. Every summer Lady Narborough went to visit
   - ☐ a. Dorian at his house on the lake.
   - ☐ b. her daughter and son-in-law.
   - ☐ c. close friends in Paris.

5. Lady Narborough wanted Dorian to
   - ☐ a. chat with Lord Henry.
   - ☐ b. sit next to her.
   - ☐ c. entertain her daughter.

Understanding the Passage

6. Apparently, Lady Narborough had never been
   - ☐ a. wealthy.
   - ☐ b. away from home.
   - ☐ c. very attractive.

7. Lady Narborough thought highly of
   - ☐ a. her son-in-law.
   - ☐ b. all her guests.
   - ☐ c. Dorian.

8. Lady Narborough's husband had apparently
   - ☐ a. died very recently.
   - ☐ b. been dead for some time.
   - ☐ c. been assassinated.

9. Lady Narborough thought life in the country was
   - ☐ a. wonderfully serene.
   - ☐ b. terribly boring.
   - ☐ c. the secret to staying young at heart.

10. Dorian agreed with Lady Narborough that her guests were
    - ☐ a. cranky and quarrelsome.
    - ☐ b. very polite.
    - ☐ c. rather dull.

Dear madam: No doubt you and Frank's friends have heard the sad fact of his death in hospital here, through his uncle, or the lady from Baltimore, who took his things. I will write you a few lines—as a casual friend that sat by his deathbed. Your son, Corporal Frank H. Irwin, was wounded near Fort Fisher, Virginia, March 25th, 1865—the wound was in the left knee, pretty bad. He was sent up to Washington, was received in ward C, Armory Square Hospital, March 28th—the wound became worse, and on the 4th of April the leg was amputated a little above the knee—the operation was performed by Dr. Bliss, one of the best surgeons in the army—he did the whole operation himself—there was a good deal of bad matter gathered—the bullet was found in the knee. For a couple of weeks afterwards he was doing pretty well. I visited and sat by him frequently, as he was fond of having me. The last ten or twelve days of April I saw that his case was critical. He previously had some fever, with cold spells. The last week in April he was much of the time flighty—but always mild and gentle. He died first of May. The actual cause of death was pyemia. Frank, as far as I saw, had everything requisite in surgical treatment, nursing, etc. He had watches much of the time. He was so good and well behaved and affectionate; I myself liked him very much. I was in the habit of coming in afternoons and sitting by him, and soothing him, and he liked to have me—liked to put his arm out and lay his hand on my knee—would keep it so a long while. Toward the last he was more restless and flighty at night—often fancied himself with his regiment—by his talk sometimes seemed as if his feelings were hurt by being blamed by his officers for something he was entirely innocent of—said, "I never in my life was thought capable of such a thing, and never was." At other times he would fancy himself talking as it seemed to children or such like, his relatives I suppose, and giving them good advice; would talk to them a long while. All the time he was out of his head not one single bad word escaped him.

Recalling Facts

1. The soldier died
   - ☐ a. on the battlefield.
   - ☐ b. in his own home.
   - ☐ c. in a hospital.

2. Frank was a
   - ☐ a. private.
   - ☐ b. corporal.
   - ☐ c. sergeant.

3. Dr. Bliss
   - ☐ a. was a top surgeon.
   - ☐ b. did the operation himself.
   - ☐ c. both a and b.

4. Pyemia was
   - ☐ a. the actual cause of death.
   - ☐ b. the name of a leg bone.
   - ☐ c. Frank's mental state just before death.

5. The narrator
   - ☐ a. was a doctor.
   - ☐ b. visited Frank regularly.
   - ☐ c. was also wounded.

Understanding the Passage

6. Frank enjoyed
   - ☐ a. his time in the hospital.
   - ☐ b. the narrator's visits.
   - ☐ c. walking the hospital ward.

7. After being wounded, Frank lived about
   - ☐ a. one week.
   - ☐ b. three days.
   - ☐ c. five weeks.

8. Apparently, the hospital staff was
   - ☐ a. poorly trained.
   - ☐ b. providing good care.
   - ☐ c. unfamiliar with treating war wounds.

9. For two weeks after his surgery, Frank
   - ☐ a. appeared to be doing well.
   - ☐ b. was difficult and hard to nurse.
   - ☐ c. lay unconscious.

10. Near the end, Frank began to
    - ☐ a. curse the war.
    - ☐ b. imagine things.
    - ☐ c. cry for his parents.

Dorothy now realized that Ugu must be treated as an enemy, so she advanced toward the corner in which he sat, saying as she went:

"I am not afraid of you, Mr. Shoemaker, and I think you'll be sorry, pretty soon, that you're such a bad man. You can't destroy me and I won't destroy you. But I'm going to punish you for your wickedness."

Ugu laughed a laugh that was not nice to hear, and then he waved his hand. Dorothy was halfway across the room when suddenly a wall of glass rose before her and stopped her progress. Through the glass she could see the magician sneering at her because she was a weak little girl, and this provoked her. Although the glass wall obliged her to halt she instantly pressed both hands to her Magic Belt and cried in a loud voice:

"Ugu the Shoemaker, by the magic virtues of the Magic Belt, I command you to become a dove!"

The magician instantly realized he was being enchanted, for he could feel his form changing. He struggled desperately against the enchantment, mumbling magic words and making magic passes with his hands. And in one way he succeeded in defeating Dorothy's purpose, for while his form soon changed to that of a gray dove, the dove was of an enormous size— bigger even than Ugu had been as a man—and this feat he had been able to accomplish before his powers of magic wholly deserted him.

And the dove was not gentle, as doves usually are, for Ugu was terribly enraged at the little girl's success. His books had told him nothing of the Nome King's Magic Belt, the Country of the Nomes being outside the Land of Oz. He knew, however, that he was likely to be conquered unless he made a fierce fight, so he spread his wings and rose in the air and flew directly toward Dorothy. The Wall of Glass had disappeared the instant Ugu became transformed.

Dorothy had meant to command the Belt to transform the magician into a Dove of Peace, but in her excitement she forgot to say more than "dove." Now Ugu was not a Dove of Peace by any means, but rather a spiteful Dove of War. His size made his sharp beak and claws very dangerous, but Dorothy was not afraid when he came darting toward her.

Recalling Facts

1. The shoemaker's name was
   - ☐ a. Dorothy.
   - ☐ b. Ugu.
   - ☐ c. Oz.

2. Dorothy was stopped by a
   - ☐ a. wall of glass.
   - ☐ b. brick wall.
   - ☐ c. net made of rope.

3. Dorothy turned Ugu into a
   - ☐ a. man.
   - ☐ b. frog.
   - ☐ c. dove.

4. Dorothy had a magic
   - ☐ a. hat.
   - ☐ b. pair of shoes.
   - ☐ c. belt.

5. As soon as Ugu became transformed, the Wall of Glass
   - ☐ a. turned into a brick wall.
   - ☐ b. shattered.
   - ☐ c. disappeared.

Understanding the Passage

6. Dorothy felt her power
   - ☐ a. could destroy Ugu.
   - ☐ b. was equal to the power of Ugu.
   - ☐ c. couldn't match the power of Ugu.

7. Ugu liked to
   - ☐ a. mock Dorothy.
   - ☐ b. destroy glass walls.
   - ☐ c. pretend he was a nice man.

8. Dorothy's spell over Ugu was
   - ☐ a. completely successful.
   - ☐ b. a partial success.
   - ☐ c. a total failure.

9. Ugu was a man of great
   - ☐ a. resourcefulness.
   - ☐ b. kindness.
   - ☐ c. physical size.

10. Dorothy apparently got her magic powers from the
   - ☐ a. Land of Oz.
   - ☐ b. Dove of Peace.
   - ☐ c. Nome King.

Town, as they called it, pleased me the less, the longer I saw it. But until our language stretches itself and takes in a new word of closer fit, town will have to do for the name of such a place as was Medicine Bow. I have seen and slept in many like it since. Scattered wide, they littered the frontier from the Columbia to the Rio Grande, from the Missouri to the Sierras. They lay stark, dotted over a planet of treeless dust, like soiled packs of cards. Each was similar to the next, as one old five-spot of clubs ● resembles another. Houses, empty bottles, and garbage, they were forever of the same shapeless pattern. More forlorn they were than stale bones. They seemed to have been strewn there by the wind and to be waiting till the wind should come again and blow them away. Yet serene above their foulness swam a pure and quiet light, such as the East never sees; they might be bathing in the air of creation's first morning. Beneath sun and stars their days and nights were immaculate and wonderful.

Medicine Bow was my first, and I took its dimensions, twenty-two buildings ● in all—one coal chute, one water tank, the station, one store, two eating houses, one billiard hall, two toolhouses, one feed stable, and twelve others that for one reason and another I shall not name. Yet this wretched husk of squalor spent thought upon appearances; many houses in it wore a false front to seem as if they were two stories high. There they stood, rearing their pitiful masquerade amid a fringe of old tin cans, while at their very doors began a world of crystal light, a land without end, a space across which Noah and Adam might come straight from Genesis. Into that space went ● wandering a road, over a hill and down out of sight, and up again smaller in the distance, and down once more, and up once more, straining the eyes, and so away.

Then I heard a fellow greet my Virginian. He came rollicking out of a door, and made a pass with his hand at the Virginian's hat. The Southerner dodged it, and I saw once more the tiger undulation of body, and knew my escort was he of the rope and the corral.

"How are you, Steve?" he said to the rollicking man.

Recalling Facts

1. The narrator compared towns like Medicine Bow to
   - ☐ a. soiled packs of cards.
   - ☐ b. neatly arranged food platters.
   - ☐ c. thriving ant colonies.

2. The narrator felt that frontier towns were
   - ☐ a. extremely rare.
   - ☐ b. all pretty much alike.
   - ☐ c. getting better and better.

3. The narrator was most impressed by the frontier's
   - ☐ a. towns.
   - ☐ b. pure air.
   - ☐ c. economic possibilities.

4. Many of the houses in Medicine Bow had
   - ☐ a. running water.
   - ☐ b. electricity.
   - ☐ c. false fronts.

5. The rollicking man tried unsuccessfully to hit the Virginian's
   - ☐ a. face.
   - ☐ b. hat.
   - ☐ c. horse.

Understanding the Passage

6. The narrator thought that describing Medicine Bow as a "town" was
   - ☐ a. inaccurate.
   - ☐ b. perfect.
   - ☐ c. demeaning.

7. The narrator traveled extensively
   - ☐ a. along the Atlantic seacoast.
   - ☐ b. through the frontier region.
   - ☐ c. by wagon and train.

8. The towns of the frontier were built
   - ☐ a. with care and attention.
   - ☐ b. over the course of several centuries.
   - ☐ c. in a hurry.

9. The narrator obviously valued
   - ☐ a. good medical care.
   - ☐ b. cultural activities.
   - ☐ c. unspoiled nature.

10. The Virginian was
    - ☐ a. very agile.
    - ☐ b. not completely sober.
    - ☐ c. a new arrival to the frontier.

My Aunt Dorothy nursed me for a week: none but she and my dogs entered the room. I had only two faint wishes left in me: one that the squire should be kept out of my sight, the other that she would speak to me of my mother's love for my father. She happened to say, musing, "Harry, you have your mother's heart."

I said, "No, my father's."

From that we opened a conversation, the sweetest I had ever had away from him, though she spoke shyly and told me very little. It was enough for me in the narrow world of my dogs' faces, and the red-leaved creeper at the window, the fir trees on the distant heath, and her hand clasping mine. My father had many faults, she said, but he had been cruelly used, or deceived, and he bore a grievous burden; and then she said, "Yes," and "Yes," and "Yes," in the voice one supposes of a ghost retiring, to my questions of his merits. I was refreshed and satisfied, like the parched earth with dews when it gets no rain, and I was soon well.

When I walked among the household again, I found that my week of seclusion had endowed me with a singular gift; I found that I could see through everybody. Looking at the squire, I thought to myself, "My father has faults, but he has been cruelly used," and immediately I forgave the squire; his antipathy to my father seemed a craze, and to account for it I lay in wait for his numerous illogical acts and words, and smiled visibly in contemplation of his rough unreasonable nature, and of my magnanimity. He caught the smile, and interpreted it.

"Grinning at me, Harry; have I made a slip in my grammar, eh?"

Who could feel any further sensitiveness at his fits of irritation, reading him as I did? I saw through my aunt; she was always in dread of a renewal of our conversation. I could see her ideas flutter like birds to escape me. And I penetrated all the others.

My aunt's maid, Davis, was shocked by my discernment of the fact that she was in love, and it was useless for her to pretend the contrary, for I had seen her granting tender liberties to Lady Ilchester's footman.

Old Sewis said gravely, "You've been to the witches, Master Harry."

Recalling Facts

1. While he was lying in bed, the narrator did not want to see
   ☐ a. his Aunt Dorothy.
   ☐ b. the squire.
   ☐ c. his dogs.

2. The narrator claimed he had the heart of his
   ☐ a. aunt.
   ☐ b. mother.
   ☐ c. father.

3. After talking to his aunt the narrator was
   ☐ a. refreshed.
   ☐ b. unsatisfied.
   ☐ c. bitterly disappointed.

4. The narrator's seclusion lasted
   ☐ a. two days.
   ☐ b. one week.
   ☐ c. three weeks.

5. The maid, Davis, was in love with
   ☐ a. a witch.
   ☐ b. the squire.
   ☐ c. the footman.

Understanding the Passage

6. The most important person in the narrator's life was
   ☐ a. his mother.
   ☐ b. his father.
   ☐ c. the squire.

7. Concerning his father, the narrator wanted to hear
   ☐ a. only good things.
   ☐ b. nothing.
   ☐ c. only bad things.

8. The squire appeared to be
   ☐ a. a close friend of the narrator's father.
   ☐ b. the narrator's best friend.
   ☐ c. rather poorly educated.

9. Harry was the
   ☐ a. narrator's first name.
   ☐ b. squire's first name.
   ☐ c. footman's first name.

10. Old Sewis thought that the narrator was
    ☐ a. not happy.
    ☐ b. still sickly.
    ☐ c. a bit crazy.

People said to her as the years passed, and she was a woman of twenty-five, then a woman of thirty, and always the same dainty Princess, "knowing" in a dispassionate way, like an old woman:

"Don't you ever think what you will do when your father is no longer with you?"

She looked at her interlocutor with that cold, elfin detachment of hers:

"No, I never think of it," she said.

She had a tiny but exquisite little house in London, and another small, perfect house in Connecticut, each with a faithful housekeeper. Two homes, if she chose. And she knew many interesting literary and artistic people. What more?

So the years passed imperceptibly. And she had that quality of the sexless fairies, she did not change. At thirty-three she looked twenty-three.

Her father, however, was aging, and becoming more and more queer. It was now her task to be his guardian in his private madness. He spent the last three years of life in the house in Connecticut. He was very much estranged, sometimes had fits of violence which almost killed the little Princess. Physical violence was horrible to her; it seemed to shatter her heart. But she found a woman a few years younger than herself, well educated and sensitive, to be a sort of nurse-companion to the mad old man. So the fact of madness was never openly admitted. Miss Cummins, the companion, had a passionate loyalty to the Princess, and a curious affection, tinged with love, for the handsome, white-haired, courteous old man, who was never at all aware of his fits of violence once they had passed.

The Princess was thirty-eight years old when her father died. And quite unchanged. She was still tiny, and like a dignified, scentless flower. Her soft brownish hair, almost the color of beaver fur, was bobbed and fluffed softly round her apple blossom face, that was modeled with an arched nose like a proud old Florentine portrait. In her voice, manner, and bearing she was exceedingly still, like a flower that has blossomed in a shadowy place. And from her blue eyes looked out the Princess's eternal laconic challenge, that grew almost sardonic as the years passed. She was the Princess, and sardonically she looked out on a princeless world.

She was relieved when her father died, and at the same time it was as if everything had evaporated around her.

Recalling Facts

1. The Princess had a house in Connecticut and
   - ☐ a. New York.
   - ☐ b. London.
   - ☐ c. Paris.

2. The Princess's father had
   - ☐ a. fits of violence.
   - ☐ b. severe headaches.
   - ☐ c. a series of mild heart attacks.

3. The nurse-companion was
   - ☐ a. younger than the Princess.
   - ☐ b. the same age as the Princess.
   - ☐ c. older than the Princess.

4. When her father died, the Princess was
   - ☐ a. 25 years old.
   - ☐ b. 30 years old.
   - ☐ c. 38 years old.

5. Physically, the Princess was
   - ☐ a. plain.
   - ☐ b. big boned.
   - ☐ c. tiny.

Understanding the Passage

6. The Princess did not have
   - ☐ a. much money.
   - ☐ b. many friends.
   - ☐ c. a husband.

7. While her father lived, the Princess
   - ☐ a. did not change much.
   - ☐ b. visited him rarely.
   - ☐ c. lacked artistic stimulation.

8. If her father's madness had become known, the Princess may have
   - ☐ a. had to restrain him.
   - ☐ b. been publicly embarrassed.
   - ☐ c. been compelled to marry.

9. The father suffered
   - ☐ a. from memory lapses.
   - ☐ b. at the hands of an uncaring daughter.
   - ☐ c. from neglect by his nurse-companion.

10. The life of the Princess seemed to be centered around
   - ☐ a. Miss Cummins.
   - ☐ b. her father.
   - ☐ c. her search for a husband.

Now it happened one day in early springtime that I, Henry Stenhouse, nineteen years of age, well and sound in mind and body, decided to commit a crime.

The crime which I contemplated was murder. For three years past I had watched the object of my pursuit; I had peered at him at night as he lay sleeping; I had crept stealthily to his home, evening after evening, waiting for a chance to kill him. I had seen him moving about on his daily business, growing fatter and sleeker, serene, sly, self-centered, absorbed in his own affairs, yet keeping a keen, shrewd eye upon strangers. For he mistrusted strangers; those who passed by him, not even noticing him, he mistrusted less than he did others who came to him with smiles and outstretched hands.

He never accepted anything from anybody. A strange step or the sound of a strange voice made him shy and suspicious. But he was cold and selfish, cold-blooded as a fish—in fact he—but I had better tell you a little more about him first. He was my enemy; I was determined to kill him, and perhaps he read it in my drawn face and sparkling eyes, for, as I stepped toward him, the first time, he turned and fled—fled straight across the Clovermead River.

And although I searched the river banks up and down and up and down again, I saw no more of him that day.

When I went home, excited, furious, I made passionate preparations to kill him. All night long I tossed feverishly in my tumbled bed, longing, aching for the morning. When the morning came I stole out of the house and bent my steps towards the river, for I had reason to believe that he lived somewhere in that neighborhood. As I crept along, the early morning sun glittered on something that I clutched with nervous fingers. It was a weapon.

This happened three years ago; I did not find him that morning although I searched until the shadows fell over meadow and thicket. That night too found me on his trail, but the calm spring moon rose over Clovermead village and its pale light fell on no scene of blood.

So for three years I trailed him and stalked him, always awaiting the moment to strike—praying for an opportunity to slay; but he never gave me one.

Recalling Facts

1. Henry Stenhouse is the
   - ☐ a. narrator.
   - ☐ b. intended victim.
   - ☐ c. sheriff.

2. The intended victim
   - ☐ a. mistrusted strangers.
   - ☐ b. was a ward of the state.
   - ☐ c. was well liked by the narrator.

3. The intended victim once escaped the narrator by fleeing across
   - ☐ a. Cumberland Gap.
   - ☐ b. the Cloverville hills.
   - ☐ c. Clovermead River.

4. The narrator stalked his intended victim for
   - ☐ a. one year.
   - ☐ b. two years.
   - ☐ c. three years.

5. The intended victim gave the narrator
   - ☐ a. a friendly smile every time they met.
   - ☐ b. a few opportunities to strike.
   - ☐ c. no opportunity to strike.

Understanding the Passage

6. The narrator's bitter feelings toward the intended victim
   - ☐ a. were fleeting.
   - ☐ b. were strong and deep.
   - ☐ c. eased after a year.

7. The intended victim had a
   - ☐ a. charming personality.
   - ☐ b. generous nature.
   - ☐ c. suspicious nature.

8. That first day, the narrator searched for his intended victim
   - ☐ a. in town.
   - ☐ b. along the riverbanks.
   - ☐ c. down the Clovermead road.

9. In this passage, the narrator's weapon was
   - ☐ a. a shotgun.
   - ☐ b. a knife.
   - ☐ c. never identified.

10. The passage gives no clues as to
    - ☐ a. where the murder would occur.
    - ☐ b. where the murder victim lived.
    - ☐ c. why the intended victim was the narrator's enemy.

Francis Ayrault had finally taken up his abode, leaving behind him the old family homestead in a Rhode Island seaside town. A series of domestic cares and watchings had almost broken him down; nothing debilitates a man of strong nature like the too prolonged and exclusive exercise of the habit of sympathy. At last, when the very spot where he was born had been chosen as a site for a new railway station, there seemed nothing more to retain him. He needed utter rest and change; and there was no one left on earth whom he loved, except a little sunbeam of a sister, the child of his father's second marriage. This little five-year-old girl, of whom he was sole guardian, had been christened by the quaint name of Hart, after an ancestor, Hart Ayrault, whose moss-covered tombstone the child had often explored with her little fingers.

The two had arrived one morning from the nearest railway station to take possession of the old brick farmhouse. Ayrault had spent the day in unpacking and in consultations with Cyrus Gerry—the farmer from whom he had bought the place, and who was still to conduct all outdoor operations. The child, for her part, had compelled her old nurse to follow her through every corner of the buildings. They were at last seated at an early supper, during which little Hart was too much absorbed in the novelty of wild red raspberries to notice, even in the most casual way, her brother's worn and exhausted look.

"Brother Frank," she remarked, as she began upon her second saucerful of berries, "I love you!"

"Thank you, darling," was his mechanical reply. She was silent for a time, absorbed in her pleasing pursuit, and then continued, "Brother Frank, you are the kindest person in the whole world! I am so glad we came here! May we stay here all winter? It must be lovely in the winter; and in the barn there is a little sled with only one runner gone. Brother Frank, I love you so much, I don't know what I shall do! I love you a thousand pounds, and fifteen, and eleven and a half, and more than a tongue can tell besides! And there are three gray kittens—only one of them is almost all white—and Susan says I may bring them for you to see in the morning."

Recalling Facts

1. Frank's old house was going to be the site of a new
   □ a. brick farmhouse.
   □ b. highway tollgate.
   □ c. railroad station.

2. Frank's sister was
   □ a. 5 years old.
   □ b. 7 years old.
   □ c. 9 years old.

3. Frank and Hart had just moved into
   □ a. a small apartment.
   □ b. an old farmhouse.
   □ c. a large mansion.

4. Hart ate two servings of
   □ a. strawberries.
   □ b. blueberries.
   □ c. raspberries.

5. In the barn Hart found
   □ a. a broken bicycle.
   □ b. three kittens.
   □ c. several old dolls.

Understanding the Passage

6. Apparently, Frank had just lost
   □ a. most of his loved ones.
   □ b. his business.
   □ c. his family's wealth.

7. At the time of his move, Frank was
   □ a. very excited.
   □ b. thoroughly tired out.
   □ c. worried about Hart.

8. Cyrus Gerry
   □ a. would help run the farm.
   □ b. was an old family friend.
   □ c. didn't like little children.

9. Frank and Hart apparently brought along
   □ a. a broken sled.
   □ b. a nurse.
   □ c. some raspberries.

10. The move to the old farmhouse
    □ a. excited Hart.
    □ b. depressed Susan.
    □ c. disappointed Cyrus Gerry.

35 *from* **Kidnapped** *by Robert Louis Stevenson*

The time I spent upon the island is still so horrible a thought to me, that I must pass it lightly over. In all the books I have read of people cast away, they had either their pockets full of tools, or a chest of things would be thrown upon the beach along with them, as if on purpose. My case was very different. I had nothing in my pockets but money and Alan's silver button; and being inland bred, I was as much short of knowledge as of means.

I knew indeed that shellfish were counted good to eat; and among the rocks of the isle I found a great plenty of limpets, which at first I could scarcely strike from their places, not knowing quickness to be needful. There were, besides, some of the little shells that we call buckies; I think periwinkle is the English name. Of these two I made my whole diet, devouring them cold and raw as I found them; and so hungry was I, that at first they seemed to me delicious.

Perhaps they were out of season, or perhaps there was something wrong in the sea about my island. But at least I had no sooner eaten my first meal than I was seized with giddiness and retching, and lay for a long time no better than dead. A second trial of the same food (indeed I had no other) did better with me and revived my strength. But as long as I was on the island, I never knew what to expect when I had eaten; sometimes all was well, and sometimes I was thrown into a miserable sickness; nor could I ever distinguish what particular fish it was that hurt me.

All day it streamed rain; the island ran like a sop; there was no dry spot to be found; and when I lay down that night, between two boulders that made a kind of roof, my feet were in a bog.

The second day, I crossed the island to all sides. There was no one part of it better than another; it was all desolate and rocky; nothing living on it but game birds which I lacked the means to kill, and the gulls which haunted the outlying rocks in prodigious number. The creek, or straits, cut off the isle from the mainland of the Ross.

Recalling Facts

1. The narrator had in his pockets
   - ☐ a. some small tools.
   - ☐ b. a map of the island.
   - ☐ c. money and a silver button.

2. The narrator thought that shellfish were
   - ☐ a. hard to find.
   - ☐ b. good to eat.
   - ☐ c. not tasty.

3. The English name for buckies was
   - ☐ a. limpets.
   - ☐ b. periwinkles.
   - ☐ c. oysters.

4. The narrator slept
   - ☐ a. in a wooden hut.
   - ☐ b. between two boulders.
   - ☐ c. under his damaged boat.

5. One thing the island did have was
   - ☐ a. ancient ruins.
   - ☐ b. wild strawberries.
   - ☐ c. game birds.

Understanding the Passage

6. The narrator felt
   - ☐ a. nearly helpless.
   - ☐ b. somewhat confident.
   - ☐ c. totally defeated.

7. Limpets were
   - ☐ a. rare.
   - ☐ b. hard to gather.
   - ☐ c. too small to eat.

8. The island apparently
   - ☐ a. lacked fruit trees.
   - ☐ b. had primitive shelters.
   - ☐ c. harbored wild animals.

9. The narrator's first meal
   - ☐ a. nearly killed him.
   - ☐ b. improved his outlook.
   - ☐ c. was well balanced.

10. The island was
    - ☐ a. a peninsula.
    - ☐ b. quite large.
    - ☐ c. rather small.

from **Little Men** *by Louisa May Alcott*

A brisk game of tag was going on in the upper entry. One landing was devoted to marbles, the other to checkers, while the stairs were occupied by a boy reading, a girl singing a lullaby to her doll, two puppies, a kitten, and a constant succession of small boys sliding down the banisters, to the great detriment of their clothes, and danger to their limbs.

So absorbed did Nat become in this exciting race, that he ventured farther and farther out of his corner; and when one very lively boy came down so swiftly that he could not stop himself, but fell off the banisters, with a crash that would have broken any head but one rendered nearly as hard as a cannonball by eleven years of constant bumping, Nat forgot himself, and ran up to the fallen rider, fearing him half dead. But the boy only winked rapidly for a second, then lay calmly looking up at the new face with a surprised "Hullo!"

"Hullo!" returned Nat, not knowing anything else to say, and thinking that form of reply both brief and easy.

"Are you a new boy?" asked the recumbent youth, without stirring.

"Don't know yet."

"What's your name?"

"Nat Blake."

"Mine's Tommy Bangs; come have a go, will you?" and Tommy got upon his legs like one suddenly remembering the duties of hospitality.

"Guess I won't, till I see whether I'm going to stay or not," returned Nat, feeling the desire to stay increase every moment.

"I say, Demi, here's a new one. Come and see to him." And the lively Thomas returned to his sport with unabated relish.

At his call, the boy reading on the stairs looked up with a pair of big brown eyes, and after an instant's hesitation, as if a little shy, he put the book under his arm, and came soberly down to greet the newcomer, who found something very attractive in the pleasant face of this slender, mild-eyed boy.

"Have you seen Aunt Jo?" he asked, as if that was some sort of important ceremony.

"I haven't seen anyone yet but you boys; I'm waiting," said Nat.

"Did Uncle Laurie send you?" asked Demi, politely, but gravely.

"Mr. Laurence did."

"He is Uncle Laurie and he always sends very nice boys."

Nat looked gratified at the remark, and smiled, in a way that made his thin face very pleasant.

Recalling Facts

1. Several small boys were
   - ☐ a. singing lullabies.
   - ☐ b. sliding down
     the banisters.
   - ☐ c. reading books.

2. Tommy Bangs asked Nat Blake if he
   - ☐ a. was a new boy.
   - ☐ b. wanted to play checkers.
   - ☐ c. would stay for dinner.

3. Demi asked Nat if he had met
   - ☐ a. Tommy Bangs.
   - ☐ b. Mr. Laurence.
   - ☐ c. Aunt Jo.

4. Nat hadn't seen anyone but
   - ☐ a. the children.
   - ☐ b. the teachers.
   - ☐ c. Demi.

5. According to Demi, Uncle Laurie only sent
   - ☐ a. little girls.
   - ☐ b. troublemakers.
   - ☐ c. nice boys.

Understanding the Passage

6. The children appeared to be having a
   - ☐ a. quiet time.
   - ☐ b. miserable time.
   - ☐ c. happy time.

7. To the other boys, Nat was
   - ☐ a. a pleasant stranger.
   - ☐ b. an unwelcome intruder.
   - ☐ c. afraid of sliding on
     the banister.

8. Tommy Bangs was
   - ☐ a. used to bumping
     his head.
   - ☐ b. polite to newcomers.
   - ☐ c. both a and b.

9. After talking to Tommy, Nat began to
   - ☐ a. grow nervous.
   - ☐ b. become frightened.
   - ☐ c. relax a little.

10. Nat was not sure he would be
    - ☐ a. allowed to slide down
      the banisters.
    - ☐ b. staying at this place.
    - ☐ c. adopted by
      Mr. Laurence.

Mr. Hazard was not happy. Like Esther he felt himself getting into a state of mind that threatened to break his spirit. He had been used to ordering matters much as he pleased. His parish at Cincinnati, being his creation, had been managed by him as though he owned it. But at St. John's he found himself less free, and was conscious of incessant criticism. He had been now some months in his new pulpit; his popular success had been marked; St. John's was overflowing with a transient audience, like a theater, to the disgust of regular pew owners. His personal influence was great, but he felt that it was not yet, and perhaps never could be, strong enough to stand the scandal of his marriage to a woman whose opinions were believed to be radical. On this point he was not left in doubt, for the mere suspicion of his engagement raised a little tempest in the pool. The stricter sect, not without reason, were scandalized. They held to their creed, and the bare mention of Esther Dudley's name called warm protests from their ranks. They flatly said that it would be impossible for Mr. Hazard to make them believe his own doctrine to be sound, if he could wish to enter into such a connection. None but a freethinker could associate with the set of freethinkers, artists and other unusual people whose society Mr. Hazard was known to affect. His marriage to one of them would give the unorthodox a hold on the parish which would end by splitting it.

One of his strongest friends, who had done most to bring him to New York and make his path pleasant, came to him with an account of what was said and thought, softening the expression so as to bear telling.

"You ought to hear about it," said he, "so I tell you; but it is between you and me. I don't ask whether you are engaged to Miss Dudley. For my own pleasure, I wish you may be. If I were thirty years younger I would try for her myself; but we all know that she has very little more religious experience than a white rosebud. I'm not strict myself, I don't mind a little looseness on the creed, but the trouble is that every old woman in the parish knows all about the family."

Recalling Facts

1. Mr. Hazard's current parish was
   - ☐ a. in Cincinnati.
   - ☐ b. St. John's.
   - ☐ c. at St. Louis.

2. Usually on Sunday the parish was
   - ☐ a. less than half full.
   - ☐ b. nearly full.
   - ☐ c. overflowing.

3. Esther Dudley's opinions were considered by many to be
   - ☐ a. radical.
   - ☐ b. conservative.
   - ☐ c. reactionary.

4. Esther Dudley was believed to be a
   - ☐ a. freethinker.
   - ☐ b. conformist.
   - ☐ c. socialist.

5. Every old woman in the parish knew all about Esther's
   - ☐ a. lack of education.
   - ☐ b. previous husbands.
   - ☐ c. family.

Understanding the Passage

6. The people of Mr. Hazard's parish were
   - ☐ a. very critical.
   - ☐ b. very open-minded.
   - ☐ c. frequently absent from church.

7. Esther apparently was not very
   - ☐ a. religious.
   - ☐ b. pretty.
   - ☐ c. well known.

8. Marrying Esther would destroy Mr. Hazard's
   - ☐ a. influence with the stricter sect.
   - ☐ b. personal religious convictions.
   - ☐ c. reputation as an honest man.

9. Mr. Hazard's present parish was located in
   - ☐ a. Ohio.
   - ☐ b. New York.
   - ☐ c. New Jersey.

10. People did not yet know for sure if Mr. Hazard really
    - ☐ a. planned to marry Esther Dudley.
    - ☐ b. enjoyed his work in the parish.
    - ☐ c. hoped to move out of town.

"Forward!" cried my uncle. Each took up his burden. Hans went first, my uncle followed, and I going third, we entered the somber gallery.

Just as we were about to engulf ourselves in this dismal passage, I lifted up my head, and through the tube-like shaft saw that Iceland sky I was never to see again!

The stream of lava flowing from the bowels of the earth in 1229 had forced itself a passage through the tunnel. It lined the whole of the inside with its thick and brilliant coating. The electric light added very greatly to the brilliancy of the effect.

The great difficulty of our journey now began. How were we to prevent ourselves from slipping down the steeply inclined plane? Happily some cracks and other irregularities served the place of steps; and we descended slowly, allowing our heavy luggage to slip on before, at the end of a long cord.

But that which served as steps under our feet, became in other places stalagmites. The lava, very porous in certain places, took the form of little round blisters. Crystals of opaque quartz, adorned with limpid drops of natural glass suspended to the roof like lusters, seemed to take fire as we passed beneath them. One would have fancied that the genies of romance were illuminating their underground palaces to receive the sons of men.

"Magnificent, glorious!" I cried, in a moment of involuntary enthusiasm. "What a spectacle, uncle! Do you not admire these variegated shades of lava, which run through a whole series of colors, from reddish brown to pale yellow, by the most insensible degrees? And these crystals—they appear like luminous globes."

"You are beginning to see the charms of travel, Master Harry," cried my uncle. "Wait a bit, until we advance farther. What we have as yet discovered is nothing—onward, my boy, onward!"

It would have been a far more correct and appropriate expression, had he said, "Let us slide," for we were going down an inclined plane with perfect ease. The compass indicated that we were moving in a southeasterly direction. The flow of lava had never turned to the right or left. It had the inflexibility of a straight line. Nevertheless, to my surprise, we found no perceptible increase in heat. This proved the theories of Humphrey Davy. More than once I examined the thermometer in silent astonishment.

Recalling Facts

1. As the group moved forward, the narrator went
   □ a. first.
   □ b. second.
   □ c. third.

2. The narrator saw the Icelandic sky
   □ a. for the first time.
   □ b. for the last time.
   □ c. everyday.

3. In 1229, the tunnel was filled with
   □ a. lava.
   □ b. crystals.
   □ c. water.

4. The Professor referred to the narrator as
   □ a. Hans.
   □ b. Master Harry.
   □ c. Humphrey Davy.

5. As the group slid down, there was no increase in
   □ a. pressure.
   □ b. the slope.
   □ c. heat.

Understanding the Passage

6. The narrator seemed to
   □ a. get sicker with every step.
   □ b. enjoy himself despite his nervousness.
   □ c. feel the heat of hardened lava.

7. The scenery inside the tunnel was
   □ a. depressing.
   □ b. unremarkable.
   □ c. spectacular.

8. The group had to move
   □ a. quickly.
   □ b. cautiously.
   □ c. independently.

9. The narrator seemed to be most impressed by the
   □ a. Professor's speed.
   □ b. Icelandic sky.
   □ c. lava crystals.

10. It was expected that
   □ a. no one could walk on the hardened lava.
   □ b. the temperature would increase in the tunnel.
   □ c. the tunnel would not veer right or left.

One fine summer day, during the time alloted us for recreation, Petroff was
led out to be flogged for some offense. The officer who was in immediate
charge of the prison had come to the guardroom, which was at the gates
of the prison, to superintend the execution of the sentence in person. This
major was held in abomination by the convicts. He made a great mistake
in treating us as he did, and by his imprudent and cruel behavior he only
embittered and irritated men who were already almost too much so. If it
had not been for the head Commandant of the Prison, he might have done
us a great deal more harm. As it was, I often wonder that not more attempts
were made to murder him. He tyrannized over us for a good many years,
and finally left the service. It is true that he was brought up before a court-
martial subsequently, but that could not take away our past sufferings and
make them undone.

The convict turned pale when he was summoned to the guardroom. As
a rule he had always submitted to his punishment without saying a word
or uttering a scream, and got up after it and walked quietly away as if he
had never so much as felt one blow; but this time he thought himself in
the right, and had made up his mind not to submit to what he considered
an injustice. As I have said before, he turned pale, and managed to slip
a sharp English shoe knife into his sleeve. It was strictly prohibited to have
knives in the prison. The prisoner who was found to be in unlawful
possession of a knife was severely punished. But as no trade or handicraft
can be carried on without a knife, those who had lost them took good care
to provide themselves with others at the first opportunity. All the convicts
rushed up to the fence. They watched anxiously through the chinks, as it
was well known that Petroff had made up his mind not to submit this time,
and to kill the major. But, fortunately for himself, at the last moment our
major got into his droshki and drove away, having asked another officer
to superintend the flogging. "God has saved his life," said the convicts.
Petroff at once renounced all ideas of murder, and lay down to be flogged.

Recalling Facts

1. The officer in charge of the flogging was a
   - ☐ a. lieutenant.
   - ☐ b. major.
   - ☐ c. colonel.

2. After being punished, Petroff usually
   - ☐ a. screamed.
   - ☐ b. walked quietly away.
   - ☐ c. wished he were dead.

3. In his shirt, Petroff hid a
   - ☐ a. gun.
   - ☐ b. club.
   - ☐ c. knife.

4. The other convicts knew that Petroff
   - ☐ a. wouldn't suffer the major's flogging.
   - ☐ b. wouldn't attempt murder.
   - ☐ c. was innocent of any wrongdoing.

5. At the last minute, the hated officer
   - ☐ a. pardoned Petroff.
   - ☐ b. drove away.
   - ☐ c. was transferred to another cellblock.

Understanding the Passage

6. The narrator thought that the officer's ill-treatment of the convicts was
   - ☐ a. understandable.
   - ☐ b. uninteresting.
   - ☐ c. unfair.

7. Apparently, the Commandant of the Prison
   - ☐ a. shared the cruel officer's views.
   - ☐ b. was more fair-minded than the major.
   - ☐ c. enjoyed floggings.

8. It was Petroff's intent to
   - ☐ a. quietly submit to the flogging.
   - ☐ b. threaten the officer.
   - ☐ c. kill the officer.

9. The other convicts were eager to
   - ☐ a. see what Petroff would do.
   - ☐ b. save the officer.
   - ☐ c. see Petroff killed.

10. Petroff's knife was
    - ☐ a. given to him by a guard.
    - ☐ b. an illegal weapon.
    - ☐ c. a harmless piece of tin.

Vereker said he would take my review of his novel upstairs with him and look at it. He did this half an hour later—I saw it in his hand when he repaired to his room. That was the moment at which, thinking to give her pleasure, I mentioned to Lady Jane that I was the author of the review. I did give her pleasure, but perhaps not quite so much as I had expected. If the author was "only me" the thing didn't seem quite so remarkable. Hadn't I had the effect rather of diminishing the luster of the article than of adding to my own? Her ladyship was subject to the most extraordinary drops. It didn't matter; the only effect I cared about was the one it would have on Vereker up there by his bedroom fire.

At dinner I watched for the signs of this impression, tried to fancy some happier light in his eyes; but to my disappointment Lady Jane gave me no chance to make sure. I had hoped she'd call triumphantly down the table, publicly demand acknowledgment that the review was as great as she claimed. The party was large—there were people from outside as well, but I had never seen a table long enough to deprive Lady Jane of a triumph. I was just reflecting in truth that this interminable board would deprive *me* of one when the guest next to me, dear woman—she was Miss Poyle, the vicar's sister, a robust unmodulated person—had the happy inspiration and unusual courage to address herself across it to Vereker, who was opposite, but not directly, so that when he replied they were both leaning forward. She inquired, artless body, what he thought of Lady Jane's "panegyric," which she had read—not connecting it however with her right-hand neighbor; and while I strained my ear for his reply I heard him, to my stupefaction, call back gaily, his mouth full of bread: "Oh it's all right—the usual twaddle!"

I had caught Vereker's glance as he spoke, but Miss Poyle's surprise was a fortunate cover for my own. "You mean he doesn't do you justice?" said the excellent woman.

Vereker laughed out, and I was happy to be able to do the same. "It's a charming article," he tossed us.

Miss Poyle thrust her chin half across the cloth. "Oh you're so deep!" she drove home.

Recalling Facts

1. Vereker read the review
   - ☐ a. in the garden.
   - ☐ b. in his room.
   - ☐ c. at his office.

2. The narrator told Lady Jane that he was the author of
   - ☐ a. the review.
   - ☐ b. a new novel.
   - ☐ c. Vereker's biography.

3. The only reaction the narrator really cared about was
   - ☐ a. Lady Jane's.
   - ☐ b. Miss Poyle's.
   - ☐ c. Vereker's.

4. The first person to ask Vereker for his reaction was
   - ☐ a. the narrator.
   - ☐ b. Lady Jane.
   - ☐ c. Miss Poyle.

5. The narrator's reaction to Vereker's opinion was one of
   - ☐ a. surprise.
   - ☐ b. delight.
   - ☐ c. outright anger.

Understanding the Passage

6. When Lady Jane first praised the review, she
   - ☐ a. didn't know the narrator had written it.
   - ☐ b. didn't know who Vereker was.
   - ☐ c. felt dissatisfied with it.

7. The narrator's reputation as a writer was apparently
   - ☐ a. not very great at present.
   - ☐ b. improved following Vereker's praise.
   - ☐ c. known to everyone in the area.

8. Apparently, Lady Jane was
   - ☐ a. painfully shy.
   - ☐ b. extremely outgoing.
   - ☐ c. a professional critic.

9. Miss Poyle's question was
   - ☐ a. ignored by Vereker.
   - ☐ b. a courageous one.
   - ☐ c. not the one the narrator wanted.

10. Vereker treated the review
    - ☐ a. in an offhanded manner.
    - ☐ b. as the best he had ever seen.
    - ☐ c. with direct and harsh condemnation.

"Second to the right, and straight on till morning."

That, Peter had told Wendy, was the way to the Neverland; but even birds, carrying maps and consulting them, could not have sighted it with these instructions. Peter just said anything that came into his head.

At first his companions trusted him implicitly, and so great were the delights of flying that they wasted time circling round church spires or any other tall objects on the way that took their fancy.

John and Michael raced, Michael getting a start.

They recalled with contempt that not so long ago they had thought ● themselves fine fellows for being able to fly round a room.

Not so long ago . . . but how long ago? They were flying over the sea before this thought began to disturb Wendy seriously. John thought it was their second sea and their third night.

Sometimes it was dark and sometimes light, and now they were very cold and again too warm. Did they really feel hungry at times, or were they merely pretending, because Peter had such a jolly new way of feeding them? His way was to pursue birds who had food in their mouths suitable for humans and snatch it from them; then the birds would follow and snatch ● it back; and they would all go chasing each other gaily for miles, parting at last with mutual expressions of goodwill. But Wendy noticed with gentle concern that Peter did not seem to know that this was rather an odd way of getting your bread and butter, not even that there are other ways.

Certainly they did not pretend to be sleepy, they were sleepy; and that was a danger, for the moment they popped off, down they fell. The awful thing was that Peter thought this funny.

"There he goes again!" he would cry gleefully, as Michael suddenly dropped ● like a stone.

"Save him, save him!" cried Wendy, looking with horror at the cruel sea far below. Eventually Peter would dive through the air, and catch Michael just before he could strike the sea, and it was lovely the way he did it; but he always waited till the last moment, and you felt it was his cleverness that interested him and not the saving of human life. Also he was fond of variety, and the sport that engrossed him one moment would suddenly cease to engage him.

Recalling Facts

1. Peter gave Wendy directions for getting to
   - ☐ a. Tomorrowland.
   - ☐ b. Fantasyland.
   - ☐ c. Neverland.

2. Peter tried to steal food from
   - ☐ a. humans.
   - ☐ b. birds.
   - ☐ c. horses.

3. Peter's actions seemed to bother
   - ☐ a. Wendy.
   - ☐ b. John.
   - ☐ c. Michael.

4. The travelers spent most of their time flying over
   - ☐ a. rugged mountains.
   - ☐ b. scorching deserts.
   - ☐ c. a cruel sea.

5. Every time Michael fell asleep he was saved by
   - ☐ a. Peter.
   - ☐ b. Wendy.
   - ☐ c. John.

Understanding the Passage

6. Peter's directions appeared to be
   - ☐ a. much too detailed.
   - ☐ b. simple and accurate.
   - ☐ c. nearly impossible to follow.

7. At first the travelers were
   - ☐ a. terribly nervous.
   - ☐ b. having a wonderful time.
   - ☐ c. highly suspicious of Peter.

8. Wendy thought that Peter should
   - ☐ a. give better directions.
   - ☐ b. find other ways to get food.
   - ☐ c. both a and b.

9. The most dangerous thing for the travelers was to
   - ☐ a. eat Peter's food.
   - ☐ b. fall asleep.
   - ☐ c. fly close to church spires.

10. Apparently, Peter loved to
    - ☐ a. tease his friends.
    - ☐ b. play only one game.
    - ☐ c. fly off on his own.

Two-thirds of the talk of drivers and conductors had been about this man Slade, ever since the day before we reached Julesburg. In order that the Eastern reader may have a clear conception of what a Rocky Mountain desperado is, in his highest state, I will reduce all this gossip to one straight-forward narrative, and present it in the following shape:

Slade was born in Illinois, of good parentage. At about twenty-six years of age he killed a man in a quarrel and fled the state. At St. Joseph, Missouri, he joined one of the early California-bound emigrant trains, and was given the post of train master. One day on the plains he had an angry dispute with one of his wagon drivers, and both drew their revolvers. But the driver was the quicker artist, and had his weapon cocked first. So Slade said it was a pity to waste life on so small a matter. He proposed that the pistols be thrown on the ground and the quarrel settled by a fist-fight. The unsuspecting driver agreed, and threw down his pistol—where-upon Slade laughed at his simplicity, and shot him dead!

He made his escape and lived a wild life for a while, dividing his time between fighting Indians and avoiding an Illinois sheriff, who had been sent to arrest him for his first murder. It is said that in one Indian battle he killed three braves with his own hand, and afterward cut their ears off and sent them, with his regards, to the chief of the tribe.

Slade soon gained a name for fearless resolution. This was sufficient merit to get him the important post of Overland division agent at Julesburg, in place of Mr. Jules. For some time, the company's horses had been stolen, and the coaches delayed, by gangs of outlaws, who were wont to laugh at the idea of any man's having the temerity to resent such outrages. Slade resented them promptly. The outlaws soon found that the new agent was a man who did not fear anything that breathed the breath of life. He made short work of all offenders. The result was that delays ceased, the company's property was let alone, and, no matter what happened or who suffered, Slade's coaches went through every time! True, in order to bring about this wholesome change, Slade had to kill several men—some say three, others say four.

Recalling Facts

1. Slade got a job in Missouri as a
   ☐ a. train master.
   ☐ b. deputy sheriff.
   ☐ c. cowboy.

2. Slade tricked his wagon driver by proposing a
   ☐ a. fistfight.
   ☐ b. coin toss.
   ☐ c. truce.

3. Slade supposedly cut off three Indians'
   ☐ a. hair.
   ☐ b. ears.
   ☐ c. fingers.

4. Slade got the job as division agent in place of
   ☐ a. Mr. Jules.
   ☐ b. Mr. Overland.
   ☐ c. Mr. Joseph.

5. Slade's coaches
   ☐ a. were often delayed.
   ☐ b. had frequent robberies.
   ☐ c. always got through.

Understanding the Passage

6. Slade was
   ☐ a. an honorable man.
   ☐ b. an outlaw.
   ☐ c. a misunderstood man.

7. In his dispute with the wagon driver, Slade was saved by his
   ☐ a. quick wits and devious thinking.
   ☐ b. honesty and friendliness.
   ☐ c. fast draw and straight shooting.

8. Slade could best be described as a
   ☐ a. simple crook.
   ☐ b. cold-blooded murderer.
   ☐ c. typical Westerner.

9. Slade always
   ☐ a. sided with the outlaws.
   ☐ b. looked out for himself.
   ☐ c. both a and b.

10. As the Overland division agent, Slade
    ☐ a. did what he was hired to do.
    ☐ b. often stole company property.
    ☐ c. constantly neglected his duties.

To Carson Chalmers, in his apartment near the square, Phillips brought the evening mail. Besides the routine correspondence there were two items bearing the same foreign postmark.

One of the incoming parcels contained a photograph of a woman. The other contained an interminable letter, over which Chalmers hung, absorbed, for a long time. The letter was from another woman, and it contained poisoned barbs, sweetly dipped in honey, and feathered with innuendoes concerning the photographed woman.

Chalmers tore this letter into a thousand bits and began to wear out his expensive rug by striding back and forth. Thus an animal from the jungle acts when it is caged, and thus a caged man acts when he is housed in a jungle of doubt.

By and by the restless mood was overcome. The rug was not an enchanted one. For sixteen feet he could travel along it; three thousand miles was beyond its power to aid.

Phillips appeared. He never entered; he invariably appeared, like a well-oiled genie.

"Will you dine here, sir, or out?" he asked.

"Here," said Chalmers, "and in half an hour." He listened glumly to the January blasts making an Aeolian trombone of the empty street.

"Wait," he said to the disappearing genie. "As I came home across the end of the square I saw many men standing there in rows. There was one mounted upon something, talking. Why do those men stand in rows, and why are they there?"

"They are homeless men, sir," said Phillips. "The man standing on the box tries to get lodging for them for the night. People come around to listen and give him money. Then he sends as many as the money will pay for to some lodging house. That is why they stand in rows; they get sent to bed in order as they come."

"By the time dinner is served," said Chalmers, "have one of those men here. He will dine with me."

"W-w-which," began Phillips, stammering for the first time during his service.

"Choose one at random," said Chalmers. "You might see that he is reasonably sober—and a certain amount of cleanliness will not be held against him. That is all."

It was an unusual thing for Chalmers to play the Caliph. But on that night he felt the inefficacy of conventional antidotes to melancholy. Something wanton and egregious, something high flavored and Arabian, he must have to lighten his mood.

Recalling Facts

1. One foreign parcel Chalmers
   received contained a
   - ☐ a. book.
   - ☐ b. diary.
   - ☐ c. photograph.

2. The letter, written by a
   woman, contained
   - ☐ a. flirtatious remarks.
   - ☐ b. poisoned barbs.
   - ☐ c. an invitation to be
     photographed.

3. Chalmers
   - ☐ a. tore up the letter.
   - ☐ b. tossed the letter into
     the fireplace.
   - ☐ c. locked the letter in
     the safe.

4. When Chalmers came home
   that night, he saw
   - ☐ a. homeless men.
   - ☐ b. striking workers.
   - ☐ c. a political rally.

5. Chalmers wanted his dinner
   guest to be
   - ☐ a. an old family friend.
   - ☐ b. a good conversationalist.
   - ☐ c. fairly sober and clean.

Understanding the Passage

6. Chalmers appeared to be a
   - ☐ a. social worker.
   - ☐ b. happy person.
   - ☐ c. wealthy man.

7. The overseas parcels
   - ☐ a. charmed Chalmers.
   - ☐ b. upset Chalmers.
   - ☐ c. were put aside
     by Chalmers.

8. Phillips was
   - ☐ a. an acquaintance.
   - ☐ b. a relative.
   - ☐ c. a servant.

9. Phillips seemed to know
   more than Chalmers about
   - ☐ a. the lodging house.
   - ☐ b. foreign women.
   - ☐ c. the life of the poor.

10. That night, Chalmers
    wanted to
    - ☐ a. mull over the letter.
    - ☐ b. try a new diversion.
    - ☐ c. try some Arabian food.

Though the family dwelt in solitude, these people held daily converse with the world. The romantic pass of the Notch is a great artery, through which the lifeblood of internal commerce is continually throbbing between Maine, on one side, and the Green Mountains and the shores of the St. Lawrence, on the other. The stagecoach always drew up before the door of the cottage. The wayfarer, with no companion but his staff, paused here to exchange a word, that the sense of loneliness might not utterly overcome him ere he could pass through the cleft of the mountain, or reach the first house in the valley. It was one of those primitive taverns where the traveler pays only for food and lodging, but meets with a homely kindness beyond all price. When the footsteps were heard, therefore, between the outer door and the inner one, the whole family rose up, grandmother, children, and all, as if about to welcome someone who belonged to them, and whose fate was linked with theirs.

The door was opened to a young man. His face at first wore the melancholy expression, almost despondency, of one who travels a wild and bleak road, at nightfall and alone, but soon brightened up when he saw the kindly warmth of his reception. He felt his heart spring forward to meet them all, from the old woman, who wiped a chair with her apron, to the little child that held out its arms to him. One glance and smile placed the stranger on a footing of innocent familiarity with the eldest daughter.

"Ah, this fire is the right thing!" cried he, "especially when there is such a pleasant circle round it. I am quite benumbed, for the Notch is just like the pipe of a great pair of bellows; it has blown a terrible blast in my face all the way from Bartlett."

"Then you are going toward Vermont?" said the master of the house, as he helped to take a light knapsack off the young man's shoulders.

"Yes; to Burlington, and far enough beyond," replied he. "I meant to have been at Ethan Crawford's tonight, but a pedestrian lingers along such a road at this. It is no matter; for, when I saw this good fire, and all your cheerful faces, I felt as if you had kindled it on purpose for me, and were waiting for my arrival."

Recalling Facts

1. The reception the young man received was
   - ☐ a. cool.
   - ☐ b. indifferent.
   - ☐ c. warm.

2. The tavern was occupied by
   - ☐ a. one old man.
   - ☐ b. a man and his wife.
   - ☐ c. a family.

3. The traveler was heading toward
   - ☐ a. Burlington, Vermont.
   - ☐ b. Bartlett, Vermont.
   - ☐ c. Portland, Maine.

4. The young man had planned to spend the night at
   - ☐ a. a camp in the Notch.
   - ☐ b. Ethan Crawford's.
   - ☐ c. the Bartlett Inn.

5. Upon seeing the traveler, the little child
   - ☐ a. became shy.
   - ☐ b. held out its arms to him.
   - ☐ c. made a strange and haunting sound.

Understanding the Passage

6. The family
   - ☐ a. enjoyed having guests.
   - ☐ b. rarely welcomed strangers.
   - ☐ c. treated visitors cautiously.

7. The Notch apparently was
   - ☐ a. physically beautiful.
   - ☐ b. cold and lonely.
   - ☐ c. both a and b.

8. A traveler staying at this family tavern was usually
   - ☐ a. overcharged.
   - ☐ b. welcomed.
   - ☐ c. ignored.

9. When he first arrived at the tavern, the young man was
   - ☐ a. cold and depressed.
   - ☐ b. anxious to move on to his next stop.
   - ☐ c. just asking directions.

10. That day, the young man had traveled
    - ☐ a. farther than he had planned.
    - ☐ b. about as far as he had planned.
    - ☐ c. fewer miles than he had planned.

45 *from* **The Saint and the Goblin** *by H. H. Munro*

The little stone Saint occupied a retired niche in a side aisle of the old cathedral. No one quite remembered who he had been, but that in a way was a guarantee of respectability—at least so the Goblin said. The Goblin was a very fine specimen of quaint stone carving, and lived up in the corbel on the wall opposite the niche of the little Saint. He was connected with some of the best cathedral folk, such as the queer carvings in the choir stalls and chancel screen, and even the gargoyles high up on the roof. All the fantastic beasts and manikins that sprawled and twisted in ● wood or stone or lead overhead in the arches or away down in the crypt were in some way akin to him; consequently he was a person of recognized importance in the cathedral world.

The little stone Saint and the Goblin got on very well together, though they looked at most things from different points of view. The Saint was a philanthropist in an old-fashioned way; he thought the world, as he saw it, was good, but might be improved. In particular he pitied the church mice, who were miserably poor. The Goblin, on the other hand, was of ● opinion that the world, as he knew it, was bad, but had better be let alone; it was the function of the church mice to be poor.

"All the same," said the Saint, "I feel very sorry for them."

"Of course you do," said the Goblin; "it's *your* function to feel sorry for them. If they were to leave off being poor you couldn't fulfill your functions; you'd be a sinecure."

He rather hoped that the Saint would ask him what a sinecure meant, but the latter took refuge in a stony silence. The Goblin might be right, but ● still, he thought, he would like to do something for the church mice before winter came on.

While he was thinking the matter over he was startled by something falling between his feet with a hard metallic clatter. It was a bright new coin; one of the cathedral jackdaws, who collected such things, had flown in with it to a stone cornice just above his niche, and the banging of the sacristy door had startled him into dropping it. Since the invention of gunpowder the family nerves were not what they once were.

Recalling Facts

1. The Saint and the Goblin
   were made of
   ☐ a. brass.
   ☐ b. wood.
   ☐ c. stone.

2. The gargoyles were located
   ☐ a. along the floor.
   ☐ b. next to the windows.
   ☐ c. up on the roof.

3. The Saint and the
   Goblin were
   ☐ a. friends.
   ☐ b. enemies.
   ☐ c. unknown to each other.

4. The Saint thought that the
   world was
   ☐ a. perfect as it was.
   ☐ b. good, but could use
      improvement.
   ☐ c. evil and very dangerous.

5. The Saint wanted to do
   something to help the
   ☐ a. church mice.
   ☐ b. Goblin.
   ☐ c. jackdaws.

Understanding the Passage

6. The cathedral must
   have been
   ☐ a. fairly plain.
   ☐ b. quite small.
   ☐ c. very ornate.

7. The Goblin appeared to be
   ☐ a. intellectual.
   ☐ b. easily confused.
   ☐ c. a philanthropist.

8. Compared to the Goblin, the
   Saint was more
   ☐ a. aggressive.
   ☐ b. optimistic.
   ☐ c. miserable.

9. The Goblin felt it was the
   Saint's job to
   ☐ a. feel sympathy for the
      church mice.
   ☐ b. hold up part of the wall.
   ☐ c. keep a stony silence.

10. The jackdaw dropped
    the coin
    ☐ a. to frighten the Saint.
    ☐ b. to wake up the Goblin.
    ☐ c. by accident.

The little old woman habitually discouraged all outbursts of youthful vanity upon the part of her son. She feared that he would get to think too much of himself, and she knew that nothing could do more harm. Great self-esteem was always passive, she thought, and if he grew to regard his qualities of mind as forming a dazzling constellation, he would tranquilly sit still and not do those wonders she expected of him. So she was constantly on the alert to suppress even a shadow of such a thing. As for him he ruminated with the savage, vengeful bitterness of a young man, and ● decided that she did not comprehend him.

But despite her precautions he often saw that she believed him to be the most marvelous young man on the earth. He had only to look at those two eyes that became lighted with a glow from her heart whenever he did some excessively brilliant thing. On these occasions he could see her glance triumphantly at a neighbor, or whoever happened to be present. He grew to plan for these glances. And then he took a vast satisfaction in detecting and appropriating them.

Nevertheless, he could not understand why, directly after a sense of this ● kind, his mother was liable to call to him to hang up his coat, her voice in a key of despair as if he were negligent and stupid in what was, after all, the only important thing in life.

"If yeh'll only get in the habit of doin' it, it'll be jest as easy as throwin' it down anywheres," she would say. "When ye pitch it down anywheres, somebody's got to pick it up, an' that'll most likely be your poor ol' mother. Yeh can hang it up yerself, if yeh'll only think." This was intolerable. He ● usually went then and hurled his coat savagely at the hook. The correctness of her position was maddening.

It seemed to him that anyone who had a son of his glowing attributes should overlook the fact that he seldom hung up his coat. It was impossible to explain this situation to his mother. She was unutterably narrow.

There came a time, too, that, even in his mother's tremendous admiration for him, he didn't entirely agree with her. He saw that his mother took pride in him in a different way from that in which he took pride in himself.

Recalling Facts

1. The little old woman feared that her son
   - ☐ a. was too violent.
   - ☐ b. might become too vain.
   - ☐ c. would never marry.

2. The son felt that his mother
   - ☐ a. did not comprehend him.
   - ☐ b. was always putting him down.
   - ☐ c. was his most important ally.

3. The little old woman often had to tell her son to
   - ☐ a. eat his meals.
   - ☐ b. brush his teeth.
   - ☐ c. hang up his coat.

4. The son found his mother's nagging
   - ☐ a. almost amusing.
   - ☐ b. meaningless.
   - ☐ c. intolerable.

5. When the son did a brilliant thing, his mother
   - ☐ a. struggled to remain impassive.
   - ☐ b. glowed with pride.
   - ☐ c. showed great displeasure.

Understanding the Passage

6. The mother feared that her son would not
   - ☐ a. obey the law.
   - ☐ b. live up to his potential.
   - ☐ c. both a and b.

7. The son knew that his mother loved his
   - ☐ a. generosity.
   - ☐ b. cleverness.
   - ☐ c. devotion.

8. The mother appeared to be
   - ☐ a. inflexible about the coat.
   - ☐ b. extremely proud of her son.
   - ☐ c. both a and b.

9. The mother and son
   - ☐ a. rarely saw each other.
   - ☐ b. spent a great deal of time together.
   - ☐ c. saw each other every other weekend.

10. The mother had
    - ☐ a. high hopes for her son.
    - ☐ b. a terrible marriage.
    - ☐ c. no other children.

Hartsel's was one of those mongrel establishments to be seen nowhere except in Southern California. Half shop, half farm, half tavern, it gathered up to itself all the threads of the life of the whole region. Indians, ranchmen, travelers of all sorts, traded at Hartsel's, drank at Hartsel's, slept at Hartsel's.

Hartsel was by no means a bad fellow—when he was sober, but as that condition was not so frequent as it should have been, he sometimes came near being a very bad fellow indeed. At such times everybody was afraid of him—wife, children, travelers, ranchmen, and all. "It was only a question of time and occasion," they said, "Hartsel's killing somebody sooner or later." And it looked as if the time were drawing near fast. But, out of his cups, Hartsel was kindly, and fairly truthful. Entertaining, too, to a degree which held many a wayfarer chained to his chair till small hours of the morning, listening to his landlord's talk. How he drifted from Alsace to San Diego County, he could hardly have told in minute detail himself; there had been so many stages and phases of the strange journey. But he had come to his last halt now. Here, in this Temecula, he would lay his bones. He liked the country. He liked the wild life, and, for a wonder, he liked the Indians. Many a good word he spoke for them to travelers who believed no good of the race, and evidently listened with polite incredulity when he would say, as he often did: "I've never lost a dollar off these Indians yet. They do all their trading with me. There's some of them I trust as high's a hundred dollars. If they can't pay this year, they'll pay next; and if they die, their relations will pay their debts for them, a little at a time, till they've got it all paid off. They'll pay in wheat, or bring a steer, maybe, or baskets or mats the women make, but they'll pay."

Hartsel's dwelling house was a long, low adobe building, with still lower flanking additions, in which were bedrooms for travelers, the kitchen, and storerooms. The shop was a separate building, of rough planks, a story and a half high, the loft of which was one great dormitory well provided with beds on the floor, but with no other article of bedroom furniture.

Recalling Facts

1. Hartsel's establishment
   - ☐ a. provided many services.
   - ☐ b. was like many places in the East.
   - ☐ c. served only Indians.

2. People feared that Hartsel would
   - ☐ a. go out of business.
   - ☐ b. kill someone.
   - ☐ c. not break up a brawl.

3. Hartsel was an excellent
   - ☐ a. poker player.
   - ☐ b. wine maker.
   - ☐ c. storyteller.

4. Hartsel planned to be buried in
   - ☐ a. Alsace.
   - ☐ b. San Francisco.
   - ☐ c. Temecula.

5. Hartsel's house was
   - ☐ a. a log cabin.
   - ☐ b. a stone hut.
   - ☐ c. an adobe building.

Understanding the Passage

6. The nature of Hartsel's establishment suggests that the area was
   - ☐ a. sparsely settled.
   - ☐ b. crowded with settlers.
   - ☐ c. just being explored.

7. Hartsel could be a problem when he was
   - ☐ a. broke.
   - ☐ b. drunk.
   - ☐ c. with Indians.

8. Apparently Hartsel was
   - ☐ a. highly reliable.
   - ☐ b. unpredictable.
   - ☐ c. unfriendly.

9. Most people in the area
   - ☐ a. hated Hartsel.
   - ☐ b. tried to cheat Hartsel.
   - ☐ c. distrusted Indians.

10. Guests at Hartsel's could expect
    - ☐ a. just the basics.
    - ☐ b. comfortable accommodations.
    - ☐ c. a boring evening.

The next morning I was up early; but I was surprised, on glancing from my window, to see that the new boarder was earlier still. She was walking down the narrow pathway, which zigzags over the fell—a tall woman, slender, her head sunk upon her breast, her arms filled with a bristle of wildflowers, which she had gathered in her morning rambles. The white and pink of her dress, and the touch of deep red ribbon in her broad drooping hat, formed a pleasant dash of color against the dun-tinted landscape. She was some distance off when I first set eyes upon her. Yet I know that this wandering woman could be none other than our arrival of last night, for there was a grace and refinement in her bearing which marked her from the dwellers of the fells. Even as I watched, she passed swiftly and lightly down the pathway, and turning through the wicket gate, at the further end of our cottage garden, she seated herself upon the bank which faced my window. Strewing her flowers in front of her, she set herself to arrange them.

As she sat there, with the rising sun at her back, and the glow of the morning spreading like an aureole around her stately and well-poised head, I could see that she was a woman of extraordinary personal beauty. Her face was Spanish rather than English in its type—oval, olive, with black, sparkling eyes, and a sweetly sensitive mouth. From under the broad straw hat two coils of blue-black hair curved down on either side of her graceful, queenly neck. I was surprised, as I watched her, to see that her shoes and skirt bore witness to a journey rather than to a mere morning ramble. Her light dress was stained, wet and bedraggled. Her boots were thick with the yellow soil of the fells. Her face, too, wore a weary expression, and her young beauty seemed to be clouded over by the shadow of inward trouble. Even as I watched her, she burst suddenly into wild weeping, and throwing down her bundle of flowers ran swiftly into the house.

Distrait as I was and weary of the ways of the world, I was conscious of a sudden pang of sympathy and grief as I looked upon the spasm of despair which seemed to convulse this strange and beautiful woman.

Recalling Facts

1. The woman was carrying
   - ☐ a. wildflowers.
   - ☐ b. bolts of cloth.
   - ☐ c. several books.

2. The woman wore a
   - ☐ a. white and pink dress.
   - ☐ b. broad drooping hat.
   - ☐ c. both a and b.

3. The woman had arrived
   - ☐ a. several weeks earlier.
   - ☐ b. the previous week.
   - ☐ c. just last night.

4. The woman's face looked
   - ☐ a. Irish.
   - ☐ b. Spanish.
   - ☐ c. English.

5. As the narrator watched the woman, she
   - ☐ a. burst into tears.
   - ☐ b. began laughing out loud.
   - ☐ c. fell to the ground.

Understanding the Passage

6. The narrator looked at the woman
   - ☐ a. with great interest.
   - ☐ b. for only a moment or two.
   - ☐ c. with disappointment.

7. The regular dwellers of the fells
   - ☐ a. were poor.
   - ☐ b. lacked great refinement.
   - ☐ c. were puzzled by the tall woman.

8. The woman's dress indicated that she
   - ☐ a. had just bathed.
   - ☐ b. was quite wealthy.
   - ☐ c. had been outside for some time.

9. The woman appeared to be
   - ☐ a. depressed.
   - ☐ b. overjoyed.
   - ☐ c. excited.

10. The narrator viewed the woman with
    - ☐ a. concern.
    - ☐ b. fear.
    - ☐ c. repulsion.

49 *from* **The Autocrat of the Breakfast Table** *by Oliver Wendell Holmes*

If you want to hear my confessions, the next thing, I said, is to know whether I can trust you with them. It is only fair to say that there are a great many people in the world who laugh at such things. I think they are fools, but perhaps you don't all agree with me.

I was born and bred, as I have told you twenty times, among books and those who knew what was in books. I was carefully instructed in things temporal and spiritual. But up to a considerable maturity of childhood I believed Raphael and Michelangelo to have been superhuman beings. The central doctrine of the prevalent religious faith of Christendom was utterly confused and neutralized in my mind for years by one of those too common stories of actual life, which I overheard repeated in a whisper. Why did I not ask? you will say. You don't remember the rosy modesty of sensitive children. The first instinctive movement of the little creatures is to make a *cache*, and bury in it beliefs, doubts, dreams, hopes, and terrors. I am uncovering one of these *caches*. Do you think I was necessarily a greater fool and coward than another?

I was afraid of ships. Why, I could never tell. The masts looked frightfully tall, but they were not so tall as the steeple of our old yellow meetinghouse. At any rate I used to hide my eyes from the sloops and schooners that were wont to lie at the end of the bridge, and I confess that traces of this undefined terror lasted very long. One other source of alarm had still more fearful significance. There was a great wooden HAND, a glove maker's sign, which used to swing and creak in the blast, as it hung from a pillar before a certain shop a mile or two outside of the city. Oh, the dreadful hand! Always hanging there ready to catch up a little boy, who would come to supper no more, nor yet to bed, whose porringer would be laid away empty thenceforth, and his half-worn shoes wait until his small brother grew to fit them.

As for all manner of superstitious observances, I used once to think I must have been particular in having such a list of them, but I now believe that half the children of the same age go through the same experiences.

Recalling Facts

1. According to the narrator, many people laugh at
   - ☐ a. confessions.
   - ☐ b. lies.
   - ☐ c. spiritual things.

2. The narrator grew up with
   - ☐ a. no parents.
   - ☐ b. plenty of books.
   - ☐ c. a severe lack of self-confidence.

3. The narrator once believed that Raphael was
   - ☐ a. a poor artist.
   - ☐ b. superhuman.
   - ☐ c. a fictitious person.

4. The narrator was afraid of
   - ☐ a. cars.
   - ☐ b. trains.
   - ☐ c. schooners.

5. The glove maker's sign was
   - ☐ a. unusually small.
   - ☐ b. a great wooden hand.
   - ☐ c. a list of prices.

Understanding the Passage

6. The narrator was
   - ☐ a. slightly reluctant to confess.
   - ☐ b. overly anxious to tell all.
   - ☐ c. someone who laughed at confessions.

7. The narrator's education was
   - ☐ a. almost nonexistent.
   - ☐ b. too narrowly focused on religion.
   - ☐ c. well-rounded.

8. In the narrator's mind, the central doctrine of Christendom was
   - ☐ a. all mixed up.
   - ☐ b. easily defended.
   - ☐ c. the sole focus of his life.

9. The narrator's fear of tall masts was
   - ☐ a. cured after childhood.
   - ☐ b. never fully understood.
   - ☐ c. equaled by his fear of church steeples.

10. The narrator was once fearful that the glove maker's sign would
    - ☐ a. drop on his head.
    - ☐ b. double in size.
    - ☐ c. grab him and take him away.

from **The Strange Case of Dr. Jekyll and Mr. Hyde** *by Robert Louis Stevenson*

Dear Lanyon, you are one of my oldest friends, and although we may have differed at times on scientific questions, I cannot remember, at least on my side, any break in our affection. There was never a day when, if you had said to me, "Jekyll, my life, my honor, my reason, depend upon you," I would not have sacrificed my left hand to help you. Lanyon, my life, my honor, my reason, are all at your mercy. If you fail me tonight, I am lost. You might suppose, after this preface, that I am going to ask you for something dishonorable to grant. Judge for yourself.

I want you to postpone all other engagements for tonight—ay, even if you were summoned to the bedside of an emperor—to take a cab, and with this letter in your hand for consultation, to drive straight to my house. Poole, my butler, has his orders; you will find him waiting your arrival with a locksmith. The door of my cabinet is then to be forced, and you are to go in alone, to open the glazed press on the left hand, breaking the lock if it be shut, and to draw out, *with all its contents as they stand,* the fourth drawer from the top or (which is the same thing) the third from the bottom. In my extreme distress of mind, I have a morbid fear of misdirecting you, but even if I am in error, you may know the right drawer by its contents: some powders, a vial and a paper book. This drawer I beg of you to carry back with you to Cavendish Square exactly as it stands.

That is the first part of the service: now for the second. You should be back long before midnight; but I will leave you that amount of margin, not only in the fear of one of those obstacles that can neither be prevented nor foreseen, but because an hour when your servants are in bed is to be preferred for what will then remain to do. At midnight, then, I have to ask you to be alone in your consulting room, to admit with your own hand into the house a man who will present himself in my name, and to place in his hands the drawer that you will have brought with you from the cabinet.

Recalling Facts

1. Lanyon was one of Jekyll's
   □ a. business partners.
   □ b. oldest friends.
   □ c. relatives.

2. Jekyll wanted Lanyon to
   □ a. postpone all his plans
      for the night.
   □ b. sacrifice his left hand.
   □ c. do something
      dishonorable.

3. Jekyll asked Lanyon to
   □ a. stay by his bedside.
   □ b. leave town.
   □ c. take a letter to his house.

4. Poole was
   □ a. Jekyll's butler.
   □ b. Lanyon's butler.
   □ c. the locksmith.

5. Lanyon was to be alone in his
   consulting room
   □ a. by seven o'clock.
   □ b. at midnight.
   □ c. at sunrise.

Understanding the Passage

6. The friendship between
   Lanyon and Jekyll was
   □ a. newly formed.
   □ b. strained by scientific
      disagreements.
   □ c. apparently a close one.

7. Jekyll's request seemed to be
   □ a. unacceptable to Lanyon.
   □ b. extremely urgent.
   □ c. not unusual.

8. It was most important that
   Lanyon
   □ a. act with extreme
      caution.
   □ b. follow Jekyll's
      instructions precisely.
   □ c. visit Jekyll the next day.

9. One thing Lanyon was not to
   do was to
   □ a. break the lock on
      the cabinet.
   □ b. rearrange the contents
      of the drawer.
   □ c. carry the drawer to
      Cavendish Square.

10. Jekyll tried to give Lanyon
    □ a. the exact combination
       to the locks.
    □ b. reasons for his request.
    □ c. plenty of time.

Answer Key

Progress Graph

Pacing Graph

Answer Key

1	1. a	2. c	3. b	4. a	5. b	6. c	7. a	8. a	9. b	10. c
2	1. a	2. a	3. b	4. c	5. b	6. a	7. c	8. c	9. a	10. a
3	1. c	2. c	3. c	4. c	5. c	6. c	7. b	8. a	9. b	10. a
4	1. a	2. b	3. a	4. c	5. a	6. b	7. c	8. c	9. b	10. a
5	1. c	2. b	3. b	4. a	5. c	6. a	7. a	8. a	9. c	10. b
6	1. b	2. a	3. b	4. c	5. c	6. c	7. b	8. b	9. a	10. a
7	1. a	2. a	3. c	4. c	5. b	6. b	7. c	8. b	9. b	10. b
8	1. a	2. c	3. b	4. a	5. a	6. b	7. c	8. a	9. a	10. b
9	1. b	2. b	3. a	4. c	5. c	6. b	7. c	8. a	9. a	10. b
10	1. c	2. a	3. c	4. b	5. b	6. c	7. c	8. a	9. a	10. b
11	1. b	2. a	3. c	4. c	5. b	6. c	7. a	8. b	9. a	10. b
12	1. b	2. a	3. b	4. c	5. b	6. a	7. b	8. b	9. c	10. b
13	1. b	2. a	3. b	4. c	5. c	6. a	7. b	8. b	9. c	10. c
14	1. a	2. c	3. a	4. a	5. a	6. c	7. a	8. b	9. a	10. b
15	1. c	2. a	3. b	4. c	5. c	6. a	7. b	8. c	9. a	10. b
16	1. a	2. c	3. b	4. c	5. b	6. b	7. a	8. c	9. a	10. b
17	1. b	2. a	3. c	4. a	5. b	6. c	7. b	8. a	9. b	10. b
18	1. c	2. b	3. a	4. b	5. c	6. a	7. a	8. a	9. c	10. a
19	1. a	2. c	3. c	4. b	5. b	6. b	7. b	8. c	9. c	10. c
20	1. c	2. b	3. c	4. a	5. b	6. a	7. c	8. b	9. b	10. c
21	1. b	2. c	3. a	4. b	5. b	6. a	7. b	8. c	9. b	10. b
22	1. b	2. b	3. a	4. c	5. b	6. a	7. b	8. c	9. a	10. a
23	1. a	2. b	3. b	4. c	5. b	6. c	7. a	8. b	9. a	10. a
24	1. b	2. a	3. c	4. a	5. b	6. c	7. b	8. c	9. a	10. c
25	1. b	2. a	3. c	4. a	5. b	6. a	7. b	8. c	9. c	10. c

26	1. c	2. a	3. b	4. c	5. c	6. a	7. b	8. a	9. c	10. b
27	1. b	2. a	3. b	4. b	5. b	6. c	7. c	8. b	9. b	10. c
28	1. c	2. b	3. c	4. a	5. b	6. b	7. c	8. b	9. a	10. b
29	1. b	2. a	3. c	4. c	5. c	6. b	7. a	8. b	9. a	10. c
30	1. a	2. b	3. b	4. c	5. b	6. a	7. b	8. c	9. c	10. a
31	1. b	2. c	3. a	4. b	5. c	6. b	7. a	8. c	9. a	10. c
32	1. b	2. a	3. a	4. c	5. c	6. c	7. a	8. b	9. a	10. b
33	1. a	2. a	3. c	4. c	5. c	6. b	7. c	8. b	9. c	10. c
34	1. c	2. a	3. b	4. c	5. b	6. a	7. b	8. a	9. b	10. a
35	1. c	2. b	3. b	4. b	5. c	6. a	7. b	8. a	9. a	10. c
36	1. b	2. a	3. c	4. a	5. c	6. c	7. a	8. c	9. c	10. b
37	1. b	2. c	3. a	4. a	5. c	6. a	7. a	8. a	9. b	10. a
38	1. c	2. b	3. a	4. b	5. c	6. b	7. c	8. b	9. c	10. b
39	1. b	2. b	3. c	4. a	5. b	6. c	7. b	8. c	9. a	10. b
40	1. b	2. a	3. c	4. c	5. a	6. a	7. a	8. b	9. b	10. a
41	1. c	2. b	3. a	4. c	5. a	6. c	7. b	8. c	9. b	10. a
42	1. a	2. a	3. b	4. a	5. c	6. b	7. a	8. b	9. b	10. a
43	1. c	2. b	3. a	4. a	5. c	6. c	7. b	8. c	9. c	10. b
44	1. c	2. c	3. a	4. b	5. b	6. a	7. c	8. b	9. a	10. c
45	1. c	2. c	3. a	4. b	5. a	6. c	7. a	8. b	9. a	10. c
46	1. b	2. a	3. c	4. c	5. b	6. b	7. b	8. c	9. b	10. a
47	1. a	2. b	3. c	4. c	5. c	6. a	7. b	8. b	9. c	10. a
48	1. a	2. c	3. c	4. b	5. a	6. a	7. b	8. c	9. a	10. a
49	1. a	2. b	3. b	4. c	5. b	6. a	7. c	8. a	9. b	10. c
50	1. b	2. a	3. c	4. a	5. b	6. c	7. b	8. b	9. b	10. c

Progress Graph (1–25)

Directions: Write your comprehension score in the box under the selection number. Then put an x on the line above each box to show your reading time and words-per-minute reading rate.

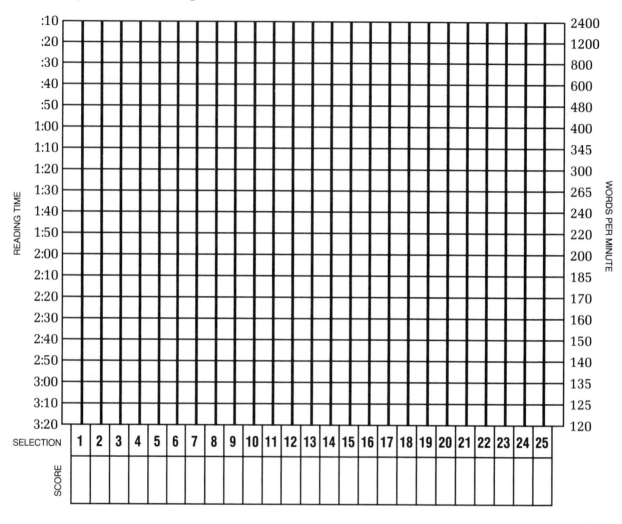

Progress Graph (26–50)

Directions: Write your comprehension score in the box under the selection number. Then put an x on the line above each box to show your reading time and words-per-minute reading rate.

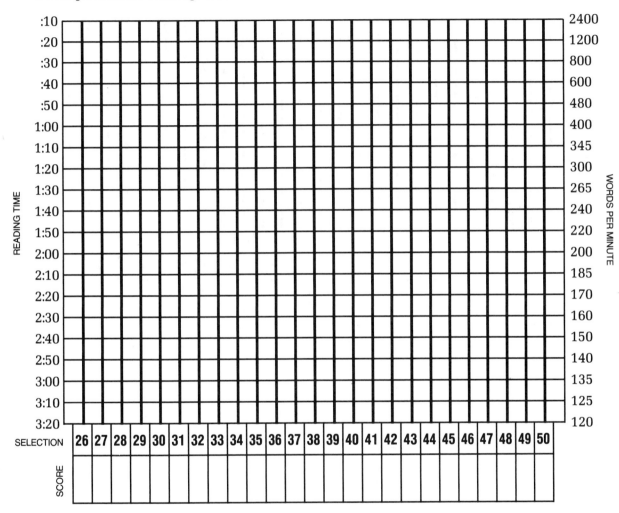

READING TIME		WORDS PER MINUTE
:10		2400
:20		1200
:30		800
:40		600
:50		480
1:00		400
1:10		345
1:20		300
1:30		265
1:40		240
1:50		220
2:00		200
2:10		185
2:20		170
2:30		160
2:40		150
2:50		140
3:00		135
3:10		125
3:20		120

SELECTION: 26 27 28 29 30 31 32 33 34 35 36 37 38 39 40 41 42 43 44 45 46 47 48 49 50

SCORE

Pacing Graph

Directions: In the boxes labeled "Pace" along the bottom of the graph, write your words-per-minute rate. On the vertical line above each box, put an x to indicate your comprehension score.

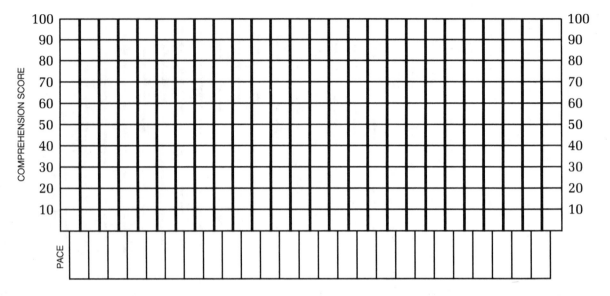